D1476087

MODERN WORLD LEADERS

Felipe Calderón

MODERN WORLD LEADERS

Michelle Bachelet	Angela Merkel
Tony Blair	Hosni Mubarak
George W. Bush	Pervez Musharraf
Felipe Calderón	Ehud Olmert
Hugo Chávez	Pope Benedict XVI
Jacques Chirac	Pope John Paul II
Hu Jintao	Roh Moo Hyun
Hamid Karzai	Vladimir Putin
Ali Khamenei	The Saudi Royal Family
Kim Jong Il	Ariel Sharon
Thabo Mbeki	Viktor Yushchenko

MODERN WORLD LEADERS

Felipe Calderón

Susan Muaddi Darraj

CHELSEA HOUSE
PUBLISHERS
An imprint of Infobase Publishing

Felipe Calderón

Chelsea House
An imprint of Infobase Publishing
132 West 31st Street
New York, NY 10001

Library of Congress Cataloging-in-Publication Data
Darraj, Susan Muaddi.
  Felipe Calderón / by Susan Muaddi Darraj.
    p. cm. — (Modern world leaders)
  Includes bibliographical references and index.
  ISBN 978-1-60413-148-2 (hardcover)
  1. Calderón Hinojosa, Felipe, 1962—Juvenile literature. 2. Mexico—Politics and
government—2000—Juvenile literature. 3. Presidents—Mexico—Juvenile literature..
I. Title. II. Series.
  F1236.9.C35D37 2008
  972.08'42092—dc22   2008014060

Text design by Erik Lindstrom
Cover design by Takeshi Takahashi

Printed in the United States of America

Bang EJB 10 9 8 7 6 5 4 3 2 1

This book is printed on acid-free paper.

TABLE OF CONTENTS

ARTHUR M. SCHLESINGER, JR.

On Leadership

Leadership, it may be said, is really what makes the world go round. Love no doubt smoothes the passage; but love is a private transaction between consenting adults. Leadership is a public transaction with history. The idea of leadership affirms the capacity of individuals to move, inspire, and mobilize masses of people so that they act together in pursuit of an end. Sometimes leadership serves good purposes, sometimes bad; but whether the end is benign or evil, great leaders are those men and women who leave their personal stamp on history.

Now, the very concept of leadership implies the proposition that individuals can make a difference. This proposition has never been universally accepted. From classical times to the present day, eminent thinkers have regarded individuals as no more than the agents and pawns of larger forces, whether the gods and goddesses of the ancient world or, in the modern era, race, class, nation, the dialectic, the will of the people, the spirit of the times, history itself. Against such forces, the individual dwindles into insignificance.

So contends the thesis of historical determinism. Tolstoy's great novel *War and Peace* offers a famous statement of the case. Why, Tolstoy asked, did millions of men in the Napoleonic Wars, denying their human feelings and their common sense, move back and forth across Europe slaughtering their fellows? "The war," Tolstoy answered, "was bound to happen simply because it was bound to happen." All prior history determined it. As for leaders, they, Tolstoy said, "are but the labels that serve to give a name to an end and, like labels, they have the least possible connection with the event." The greater the leader, "the more conspicuous the inevitability and the predestination of every act he commits." The leader, said Tolstoy, is "the slave of history."

Determinism takes many forms. Marxism is the determinism of class. Nazism the determinism of race. But the idea of men and women as the slaves of history runs athwart the deepest human instincts. Rigid determinism abolishes the idea of human freedom—the assumption of free choice that underlies every move we make, every word we speak, every thought we think. It abolishes the idea of human responsibility, since it is manifestly unfair to reward or punish people for actions that are by definition beyond their control. No one can live consistently by any deterministic creed. The Marxist states prove this themselves by their extreme susceptibility to the cult of leadership.

More than that, history refutes the idea that individuals make no difference. In December 1931, a British politician crossing Fifth Avenue in New York City between 76th and 77th streets around 10:30 P.M. looked in the wrong direction and was knocked down by an automobile—a moment, he later recalled, of a man aghast, a world aglare: "I do not understand why I was not broken like an eggshell or squashed like a gooseberry." Fourteen months later an American politician, sitting in an open car in Miami, Florida, was fired on by an assassin; the man beside him was hit. Those who believe that individuals make no difference to history might well ponder whether the next two decades would have been the same had Mario Constasino's car killed Winston Churchill in 1931 and Giuseppe Zangara's bullet killed Franklin Roosevelt in 1933. Suppose, in addition, that Lenin had died of typhus in Siberia in 1895 and that Hitler had been killed on the western front in 1916. What would the twentieth century have looked like now?

For better or for worse, individuals do make a difference. "The notion that a people can run itself and its affairs anonymously," wrote the philosopher William James, "is now well known to be the silliest of absurdities. Mankind does nothing save through initiatives on the part of inventors, great or small, and imitation by the rest of us—these are the sole factors in human progress. Individuals of genius show the way, and set the patterns, which common people then adopt and follow."

Leadership, James suggests, means leadership in thought as well as in action. In the long run, leaders in thought may well make the greater difference to the world. "The ideas of economists and political philosophers, both when they are right and when they are wrong," wrote John Maynard Keynes, "are more powerful than is commonly understood. Indeed the world is ruled by little else. Practical men, who believe themselves to be quite exempt from any intellectual influences, are usually the slaves of some defunct economist. . . . The power of vested interests is vastly exaggerated compared with the gradual encroachment of ideas."

But, as Woodrow Wilson once said, "Those only are leaders of men, in the general eye, who lead in action. . . . It is at their hands that new thought gets its translation into the crude language of deeds." Leaders in thought often invent in solitude and obscurity, leaving to later generations the tasks of imitation. Leaders in action—the leaders portrayed in this series—have to be effective in their own time.

And they cannot be effective by themselves. They must act in response to the rhythms of their age. Their genius must be adapted, in a phrase from William James, "to the receptivities of the moment." Leaders are useless without followers. "There goes the mob," said the French politician, hearing a clamor in the streets. "I am their leader. I must follow them." Great leaders turn the inchoate emotions of the mob to purposes of their own. They seize on the opportunities of their time, the hopes, fears, frustrations, crises, potentialities. They succeed when events have prepared the way for them, when the community is awaiting to be aroused, when they can provide the clarifying and organizing ideas. Leadership completes the circuit between the individual and the mass and thereby alters history.

It may alter history for better or for worse. Leaders have been responsible for the most extravagant follies and most monstrous crimes that have beset suffering humanity. They have also been vital in such gains as humanity has made in individual freedom, religious and racial tolerance, social justice, and respect for human rights.

There is no sure way to tell in advance who is going to lead for good and who for evil. But a glance at the gallery of men and women in MODERN WORLD LEADERS suggests some useful tests.

One test is this: Do leaders lead by force or by persuasion? By command or by consent? Through most of history leadership was exercised by the divine right of authority. The duty of followers was to defer and to obey. "Theirs not to reason why/Theirs but to do and die." On occasion, as with the so-called enlightened despots of the eighteenth century in Europe, absolutist leadership was animated by humane purposes. More often, absolutism nourished the passion for domination, land, gold, and conquest and resulted in tyranny.

The great revolution of modern times has been the revolution of equality. "Perhaps no form of government," wrote the British historian James Bryce in his study of the United States, *The American Commonwealth*, "needs great leaders so much as democracy." The idea that all people should be equal in their legal condition has undermined the old structure of authority, hierarchy, and deference. The revolution of equality has had two contrary effects on the nature of leadership. For equality, as Alexis de Tocqueville pointed out in his great study *Democracy in America*, might mean equality in servitude as well as equality in freedom.

"I know of only two methods of establishing equality in the political world," Tocqueville wrote. "Rights must be given to every citizen, or none at all to anyone . . . save one, who is the master of all." There was no middle ground "between the sovereignty of all and the absolute power of one man." In his astonishing prediction of twentieth-century totalitarian dictatorship, Tocqueville explained how the revolution of equality could lead to the *Führerprinzip* and more terrible absolutism than the world had ever known.

But when rights are given to every citizen and the sovereignty of all is established, the problem of leadership takes a new form, becomes more exacting than ever before. It is easy to issue commands and enforce them by the rope and the stake, the concentration camp and the *gulag*. It is much harder to use argument and achievement to overcome opposition and win consent. The Founding Fathers of the United States understood the difficulty. They believed that history had given them the opportunity to decide, as Alexander Hamilton wrote in the first Federalist Paper, whether men are indeed capable of basing government on "reflection and choice, or whether they are forever destined to depend . . . on accident and force."

Government by reflection and choice called for a new style of leadership and a new quality of followership. It required leaders to be responsive to popular concerns, and it required followers to be active and informed participants in the process. Democracy does not eliminate emotion from politics; sometimes it fosters demagoguery; but it is confident that, as the greatest of democratic leaders put it, you cannot fool all of the people all of the time. It measures leadership by results and retires those who overreach or falter or fail.

It is true that in the long run despots are measured by results too. But they can postpone the day of judgment, sometimes indefinitely, and in the meantime they can do infinite harm. It is also true that democracy is no guarantee of virtue and intelligence in government, for the voice of the people is not necessarily the voice of God. But democracy, by assuring the right of opposition, offers built-in resistance to the evils inherent in absolutism. As the theologian Reinhold Niebuhr summed it up, "Man's capacity for justice makes democracy possible, but man's inclination to justice makes democracy necessary."

A second test for leadership is the end for which power is sought. When leaders have as their goal the supremacy of a master race or the promotion of totalitarian revolution or the acquisition and exploitation of colonies or the protection of greed and privilege or the preservation of personal power, it is likely that their leadership will do little to advance the cause of humanity. When their goal is the abolition of slavery, the liberation of women, the enlargement of opportunity for the poor and powerless, the extension of equal rights to racial minorities, the defense of the freedoms of expression and opposition, it is likely that their leadership will increase the sum of human liberty and welfare.

Leaders have done great harm to the world. They have also conferred great benefits. You will find both sorts in this series. Even "good" leaders must be regarded with a certain wariness. Leaders are not demigods; they put on their trousers one leg after another just like ordinary mortals. No leader is infallible, and every leader needs to be reminded of this at regular intervals. Irreverence irritates leaders but is their salvation. Unquestioning submission corrupts leaders and demeans followers. Making a cult of a leader is always a mistake. Fortunately hero worship generates its own antidote. "Every hero," said Emerson, "becomes a bore at last."

The single benefit the great leaders confer is to embolden the rest of us to live according to our own best selves, to be active, insistent, and resolute in affirming our own sense of things. For great leaders attest to the reality of human freedom against the supposed inevitabilities of history. And they attest to the wisdom and power that may lie within the most unlikely of us, which is why Abraham Lincoln remains the supreme example of great leadership. A great leader, said Emerson, exhibits new possibilities to all humanity. "We feed on genius. . . . Great men exist that there may be greater men."

Great leaders, in short, justify themselves by emancipating and empowering their followers. So humanity struggles to master its destiny, remembering with Alexis de Tocqueville: "It is true that around every man a fatal circle is traced beyond which he cannot pass; but within the wide verge of that circle he is powerful and free; as it is with man, so with communities." ●

1

Charges of Corruption

IT WAS NOT THE FIRST TIME IN MEXICO'S HISTORY THAT GOVERNMENT officials were dueling over their differences. It may have been the first time, however, that they were actually exchanging blows on the floor of the congressional building.

Felipe de Jesús Calderón Hinojosa, of the Partido Acción Nacional, or National Action Party (PAN), was scheduled to be inaugurated as president of Mexico in three days. The Mexican constitution specifically stated that the president should be inaugurated in the Chamber of Deputies, Congress's lower house, before members of Congress. However, the Partido de la Revolución Democrática, or Party of the Democratic Revolution (PRD), had publicly sworn that it would not allow Calderón's inauguration to take place. The PAN had tampered with the vote, it alleged, and Calderón's victory was fraudulent. The PRD demanded a recount. Until the vote was recounted, it insisted, Mexico still did not have a legitimate successor to Vicente Fox.

Fistfights broke out in the congressional chambers, and members of the government disputed and debated the election results. Finally, the PAN seized control of the congressional floor. PAN's party members even maintained their control by sleeping on the floor overnight! With only three days to go until the inauguration, nobody knew for sure what would happen. Foreign governments and heads of state, including the United States, watched Mexico carefully. Only one thing was certain: the Mexican government had never appeared more in disarray than it did now.

Charges of corruption are nothing new in Mexican, or world, politics. Perhaps Calderón's victory would not have raised eyebrows had his main opponent, Andrés Manuel López Obrador of the PRD, not been so popular. The mayor of Mexico City from 2000 to 2005, Obrador was seen as a champion of the people, a politician who cared for the rights of those who were often voiceless. Most dramatically, in 1996, he took part in a demonstration against the Pemex oil company. Pemex's production and drilling were impacting the environment of many poor locals, especially the native Indian population who often found their needs overlooked by the government. Police brutally broke up the demonstration, and Obrador himself was injured. The news media showed pictures of him covered in blood, having been beaten up for his efforts, and he was quickly hailed as a politician with a conscience. That kind of reputation is difficult to defeat, especially by someone as soft-spoken as Calderón.

In fact, the presidential race between Calderón and Obrador was the closest in Mexican history. (A third candidate, Roberto Madrazo of the Partido Revolucionario Institucional, or PRI, was not considered a serious contender.) Calderón was declared the winner by only 0.58 percentage points, the slimmest margin of victory ever (Calderón gained 15,000,284 votes, or

Andrés Manuel López Obrador *(above)*, an accomplished and successful politician, was Felipe Calderón's greatest rival for the Mexican presidency. As one of Mexico City's most effective mayors, Obrador's popularity made him a formidable opponent in the presidential race. When the results of the election were announced, many people were surprised Calderón had won.

35.89 percent of the vote, as opposed to Obrador's 14,756,350, or 35.31 percent). The Federal Electoral Institute declared Calderón the winner on July 6, 2006, after the final count. However, the number of demonstrations that took place, led by Obrador and others of the PRD, forced the issue to be turned

FISTFIGHTS DETERMINED WHO WOULD CLAIM VARIOUS SECTIONS.

over to the Federal Electoral Tribunal. During its investigation, which did not end until September 2006, two months later, the tribunal examined the election results and attempted to certify and validate them.

Calderón and Obrador each declared himself the winner of the election. Obrador and the PRD demanded a full recount of all votes. In August, the tribunal determined that there was no validity to this request. It did find, however, that a recount in a small number of the voting districts was justified. It conducted the recount, and in September announced that neither fraud nor corruption had occurred. Its ruling cemented Calderón's victory. It also opened the door wide open for chaos to storm in.

The swearing in of the president of Mexico must take place on the congressional floor. The PRD swore that it would not allow this to happen, and its members camped out throughout several nights to claim sections of the chamber room. In fact, Obrador staged his own inauguration ceremony in Mexico City's main square, "declaring himself legal president and promising to run a parallel administration," reporter James Hider wrote. PAN members retaliated and also tried to claim sections of the chamber room. Fistfights determined who would claim various sections. Reporter John Ross wrote that the fighting included "punches, pepper gas, hair-pulling, hammerlocks, tossed soft drinks, torn suits and bloody noses."

Amidst the mini boxing matches on the congressional floor, President Vicente Fox made an interesting move. Although Calderón had not been his choice for successor (he had favored Interior Secretary Santiago Creel), Fox wanted the transition of power to proceed smoothly, so he arranged to appear on television the night before the scheduled

When the decision of the elections tribunal was announced, Calderón celebrated with his supporters and held up a newspaper with the headline, "YES, Calderón, elected unanimously." Tensions over election results had turned the country's government upside down, as a rival party struggled to prevent Calderón from being inaugurated as president.

inauguration, on November 30, around midnight. During the brief television segment, with Calderón at his side, Fox addressed the Mexican nation from Los Pinos, the Mexican residence of the president. A voice off camera read the oath to

Calderón, who swore to defend the constitution. Fox handed the presidential band to a soldier, who then handed it to Calderón. Power was thus transferred in this way.

Finally, shortly before the official inauguration was to take place on December 1, the PAN succeeded in roughing its way to a majority of the space. Calderón, who now had the protection of the Presidential Guard because he had been sworn in the night before, entered the chamber quickly, pinned on the presidential sash himself, took the oath, gave a brief speech, then exited.

The whole ceremony took less than five minutes.

During the entire time, PRD members shouted their opposition and waved banners proclaiming him a fraud and the election illegal. During the inauguration, thousands of people protested around the country, especially in the poor southern states where Obrador had been popular. Police and the military were used to control the protestors.

It was in this sinister, unpromising manner that Felipe Calderón would begin the six-year term of his presidency over a country that did not seem to want him.

2

Ancient History, Deep Roots

THE HISTORY OF CIVILIZATION IN MEXICO PRIOR TO THE "DISCOVERY" OF the New World by Christopher Columbus is known as the pre-Columbian era, which spans several thousand years. Human life in Mexico can be traced as far back as 11,000 B.C. Scientists and historians believe that humans crossed over into the northern American land mass from Asia a few thousand years earlier, when the Bering Strait was a small strip of land connecting these two continents during the Ice Age. Later, when the ice masses melted, this land bridge became submerged by water, cutting people off and allowing Asia's and North America's civilizations to develop separately from one another.

Many of these ancient peoples headed south and continued into what is now known as South America. Many settled in modern-day Central America and Mexico, and over the next several thousand years, established a complex and advanced civilization.

While the early people were hunters, it is apparent that once maize, or corn, was able to be grown, the early Mexicans became an agricultural society. They formed communities and began developing social rules, customs, and traditions.

Their societies formed what is known as Mesoamerica, and they occupied land that extends beyond Mexico's current borders. The Mesoamerican border stretched far up into the United States' southern border, into Texas and California, and down south into current-day Central American nations, such as Guatemala and Honduras.

THE GREAT TRIBES OF ANCIENT MEXICO

The three most significant native tribes of Mesoamerica were the Olmecs, the Maya, and the Aztecs.

The Olmec tribe established itself in Mexico around 1000 B.C., or roughly 2,500 years before Columbus landed in the Americas. In *A Brief History of Mexico*, Lynn Foster wrote that the Olmec is "the mother culture of Mesoamerica" because it paved the way for many that followed. However, while the Olmec made significant advances in pottery, architecture, and astronomy, among many other things, they are remembered for some of their spiritual rituals, which included human sacrifice.

The Mayan culture flourished between A.D. 600 and 900. The Maya tribe achieved tremendous strides in many fields. Primarily an agricultural society, they farmed maize and other staple crops. Their intellectual achievements include developing a system of writing, in hieroglyphs, and a lunar calendar that scientists have found to be quite accurate. Intellectually, the Maya were a great force. In mathematics, for example, they developed the concept of zero, which allowed them to make great advances in computation and science. Archaeologists have discovered actual books created by the Maya on various topics and subjects: poetry, history, astronomy, and religion.

LIFE WAS DIFFICULT FOR
THE AVERAGE CITIZEN, AND WORSE
FOR THE LOWER CLASSES.

The class system was highly developed in Mayan culture. The kings and nobility lived well, and their dictates went unquestioned. Priests also held a central place of authority. The priests studied the stars and constellations to determine what the gods wanted them to do; they read the signs in the sky and interpreted them, passing on their knowledge to the kings and other rulers. Because of this divine knowledge, they held a privileged place in society. Writing in the sixteenth century, a Spanish clergyman described the role of the high priest in the ancient Mayan culture: "the lords made him presents and all the priests of the towns brought contributions to him. . . In him was the key of their learning," according to Foster.

In contrast, life was difficult for the average citizen, and worse for the lower classes, as it was for all peasants in Mesoamerican civilization. They were used to build the great structures of ancient Mexico, the towering and expansive pyramids and temples, all of which have come to represent the Mayan civilization to people today.

The Aztecs

The Aztecs built a great empire across ancient Mexico, headquartered in Tenochtitlán, their capital city built upon a lake in central Mexico, on the current-day site of Mexico City.

The Aztecs were originally nomads. In the Aztec view of their own history, they believed that their ancestors had witnessed an eagle devour a serpent. (This symbol is on the modern-day flag of Mexico.) The event was a signal that their travels had ended and a divine sign for them to settle on the land, which they did around A.D. 1200, in the Valley of Mexico.

Similar to ancient Egyptian pyramids, Mayan temples on the Yucatan peninsula *(above)* have become one of the most popular tourist attractions in Mexico. Thought to be the earliest, and most highly developed, civilization in the Western hemisphere, the Mayans made advancements in language, astrology, mathematics, and architecture.

There, they began to build the most complex and powerful Mesoamerican society to date.

Most Aztecs referred to themselves as Toltecs, which means "craftsmen," because they developed highly refined skills for building, weaving, fashioning weapons, and other trades. As their skills developed, they began to form alliances with other nearby tribes. Their social system also became quite complex, forming a class system with an inflexible structure. Kings were almost deities, while common people had to remember their inferior place (in fact, there were laws punishing commoners for attempting to dress like kings).

Soon, under various kings, they began to conquer other tribes and expand their own. The Aztecs were fierce warriors who suppressed their neighboring tribes, incorporating their land into their own empire. During this time of conquest, in the late 1300s and early 1400s, the population of the major cities swelled. The city of Tenochtitlán grew dramatically, to the point that Aztec scientists even built an aqueduct to bring water into the city to serve its inhabitants.

The Aztec empire is also referred to as the Aztec Triple Alliance because of its incorporation of three major city-states: Tenochtitlán, Texcoco, and Tlacopan. This alliance was formed in 1428. All three city-states were located in the Valley of Mexico, a region in central Mexico surrounded by volcanoes and mountains. All tributes collected by the Aztec government was distributed among these three city-states: Tenochtitlán and Texcoco each collected two-fifths, and Tlacopan, which was much smaller, collected one-fifth.

THE SPANISH CONQUEST, 1521

Lynn Foster wrote that Spain, in the early 1500s, had "the greatest war machine in all of Europe." There are many historical reasons for this.

While Europe was in its Dark Ages, in the medieval era, the Muslim empire in the Middle East and North Africa flourished. Islam eventually spread into southern Spain, also known as Andalusia, in A.D. 711, and by A.D. 720 Muslims ruled most of the peninsula of Spain. They attempted to expand northward but were stopped in a battle by the French king Charlemagne. While the time of Muslim, or Moorish, rule in Spain is generally regarded as a "golden era" because of the tolerance shown by Muslims for Christians and Jews, and the general flourishing of the arts, literature, and civilization, Christian resistance to Muslim rule slowly grew. By the end of the 1400s, the Muslim empire in Spain was in peril, and by 1492, its last grasp on Spain had been loosened.

The year 1492 was also when Christopher Columbus set sail on his voyage to find a new route to the Indies, or India. Spain had just been through many years of internal struggle to rid itself of the Moors, and now it needed to find new sources of wealth. Columbus was sure he could find a new way to reach the wealthy Indies, and once King Ferdinand and Queen Isabella's finances were able, they financed his trip.

What he found disappointed him at first. There were no great treasures of gold and jewels, just scores of hard-working people speaking a language he did not understand. However, as he continued to explore, he realized he had found something that went beyond his highest hopes: a new nation, with vast unmined resources.

The fact was that Columbus mistakenly thought he had reached the Indies and thus called the inhabitants "Indians." He and his fleet had actually landed in Haiti and "discovered" the Americas, an enormous landmass that Europeans never even realized existed. He had discovered more than a fast route to India and gold: he had stumbled upon a whole new world.

A triumphant Columbus returned to his patron king and queen with six of these natives; exotic animals, including parrots; and, most important, gold. For Ferdinand and Isabella, who had bankrupted Spain in their attempt to unify it under the banner of Christianity, this was a very welcome sight. In fact, they interpreted it as a sign from God, as a reward for having rescued Spain from Moorish domination.

The Spaniards looked next to the land west of the Gulf of Mexico as they continued reaching inward, grabbing as much territory as possible. Again, the Spaniards were shocked not just to discover new land, but to see that this land had a

When Columbus returned to Spain from the New World, his discovery amazed and surprised his patrons, King Ferdinand and Queen Isabella. Seeing Columbus's gifts of gold and exotic animals from the Americas, the Spanish government quickly decided they would exploit the resources of this new land for themselves.

people, and that these people had an ancient culture. It was a parallel world, but in their eyes, it was bequeathed to them by God.

While Montezuma determined, through his test, that the Spaniards were humans, the Spaniards unfortunately did not have the same feeling toward the Indians. To the Spaniards, the native Indians of Mexico, and of the New World in general, were subhumans, a race of people to be conquered rather than embraced. It is important to remember that the Spaniards were still recovering from their exhausting religious war, and so they considered the New World to be God's gift to them, to do with it as they saw fit.

The first thing the Spaniards decided to do with the Indians of the Caribbean and Central America was to exploit them. The next thing they determined to do was to convert them to Christianity. And they continued looking for land to conquer.

HERNÁN CORTÉS: BRILLIANT BUT BRUTAL

Hernán Cortés, a soldier looking for a fortune, landed in the new world in 1504. By then, the Spaniards already occupied the Caribbean islands, though Mexico, farther inland, was yet undiscovered.

Cortés had heard about Columbus's great discovery and, like many others, wanted to seek wealth and personal fortune, since his military career was not profitable. In the Americas, like many other Spaniards, he was disappointed. There was some gold but not enough for everyone, and most of the gold resources had been tapped by those who had arrived earlier.

Earlier expeditions had reported a landmass in the Yucatan, but it had not been explored. Cortés, a clever and insightful businessman, sniffed an opportunity. He knew the Spanish government wanted to establish a colony in the Yucatan, although nobody at that point could have suspected that the Yucatan was actually connected to a much larger, and richer, landmass: that of modern Mexico.

Cortés, who was thirty-four years old, raised a small army of 500 and received a commission from the Spanish governor of Cuba, Diego Velásquez. He launched an expedition, intent on his ultimate goal: the hunt for treasure. As he prepared his ships and soldiers, he learned that Velásquez was reconsidering his decision. Cortés knew he had to act quickly; he poured all his remaining finances into the expedition and sailed from Cuba in a hurry before the governor could change his mind. Some reports say he stole all the meat in the town and set out to sail before anyone could stop him. Whether the story is true or a legend built around Cortés, the fact remains that his ingenuity and cunning certainly led to his stunning success in conquests.

"With no prior experience commanding soldiers, much less an expedition, Cortés would nonetheless succeed where his predecessors had failed," wrote Foster. "His gambling instincts, his audacity, his intelligence, and his consuming desire for glory would enable him to defeat a nation of millions with soldiers numbering in the hundreds." In many ways, however, he must have known that this expedition was going to be a major one in his career.

Cortés and his fleet landed on the coast of the Yucatan Peninsula in 1517. Legend has it that the Aztec emperor Montezuma II (also known as Moctezuma) was not sure whether these white-skinned men were gods or humans. He created a test to determine their status. He sent messengers with gifts of food: some of the food was grains, and the other offering was food sprinkled with human blood. The sailors chose the first offering, which included, according to Lynn Foster, "tortillas, turkey, guavas, and avocados, revealing their humanity in the process."

Perhaps it was with relief that Montezuma understood that he was dealing with humans, not gods. The gods, after all, preferred human sacrifice and would have chosen the food that had been sprinkled with human blood. Little did he know that these white-skinned humans would wreak more destruction than anything he could have imagined from even the fiercest gods in the Aztec pantheon.

When the Spanish arrived in Mexico, the native Indian population was diverse; many tribes coexisted, though not peacefully. While the Spanish use of brutality against the native Indians is infamous in world history, the Indian population had already suffered tremendously under the rule of other tribes. The Aztecs were the dominant culture then, because of the Aztec Triple Alliance, and they ruled in aggressive ways. Brian R. Hamnett, in *A Concise History of Mexico*, said that "Aztec hegemony in central and southern Mexico during the fifteenth century had already accustomed the population to subordination, assimilation, and strategies of survival." Foster said, "The Aztecs were intimidating. Every adult male received military training and military success was a means to social advancement for both commoners and nobles." She adds that "the Spaniards found them sophisticated and brave in battle."

The main capital of the Aztec empire, Tenochtitlán, was an enormous city, though the empire was not held together tightly. Furthermore, because the Aztecs had brutally repressed other tribes in their empire, they had many enemies. Those enemies were willing to help the white-skinned foreigners who had landed on their shores.

The situation was perfect for a foreign conquest.

CORTÉS'S CONQUEST

Historians agree that Cortés intended to intimidate the local tribes, and he did so successfully. He used his arsenal of weapons, including canons, even on friendly tribes. After he won a small battle with one tribe of Tabasco Indians, they gave him a slave girl, Doña Malintzin, later named "Marina," who spoke the local languages and served as Cortés's interpreter. Cortés also encountered Jerónimo de Aguilar, a Spaniard who had lived in the area for nine years and had become immersed in the Mayan culture; Aguilar also helped translate for Cortés's expedition.

With these two interpreters, Cortés could negotiate with tribes he encountered, and where he could not negotiate, he could defeat in battle. Foster said, "Although he found the local cotton armor provided adequate protection against obsidian-tipped arrows and spears, Cortés realized the awesome psychological impact steel armor made on the Indians and so continued to use it." Montezuma's messengers described the Spaniards and their cannons to him: "The noise weakened one, dizzied one. Something like a stone came out of their weapons in a shower of fire and sparks. The smoke was foul; it had a sickening, fetid smell." The envoys also described the visitors, who traveled on horseback, as beasts with "two heads and six legs."

Cortés also realized that many other tribes did not like the Aztecs. According to one source, "Cortez made over 200,000 allies, including the Tlaxcala, who became his closest allies after being defeated by the Spaniards," as stated on Web site MexOnline.com.

Cortés did not know this at first, but his arrival in Mexico coincided with an Aztec religious prediction. Priests had foretold that Quetzalcoatl, a major Aztec god, would return in human form to Mexico to reclaim his kingdom. Aztecs believed Quetzalcoatl was light-skinned and bearded, which is perhaps why Cortés was confused for him. The Aztecs, according to the myth, were supposed to greet the return of the great god with pomp and ceremony. Cortés eventually realized this fortunate coincidence, perhaps as he marched to Tenochtitlán to confront Montezuma.

The march to Tenochtitlán was long, and Montezuma was updated on Cortés's progress by his spies. At several points, Montezuma sent gifts of gold to Cortés, hoping he would retreat (by now, surely he had realized that Cortés and his light-skinned army were bad news), but the gold only fueled Cortés's

CONQVISTA DE MEXICO POR CORTES. №7

Sightings of abnormal activity—a comet, a temple to the god of war destroyed by flames, and a large lake boiling and flooding the local area—frightened the Aztecs and worried their king, Montezuma. Royal soothsayers interpreted these signs as the coming of the fall of the Aztec empire, and the Spaniards later fulfilled the prophecy when, led by Hernán Cortés, they seized control of Tenochtitlan, the Aztec capitol *(above)*.

intent to find Tenochtitlán. Along the way, he captured towns, including the Aztec city of Cholula. Cortés later wrote that he and his soldiers, numbering in the hundreds, killed 3,000 people in a matter of two hours, although historians estimate the number murdered to be between 5,000 and 10,000, according to Foster.

He reached the capital city of the Aztecs in November of 1519, where, indeed, Montezuma welcomed him as Quetzalcoatl. However, Montezuma's mistake was actually in how he welcomed Cortés. He sent the Spaniard gifts of gold, including one piece that Cortés later described, as stated by Foster, as "a large gold wheel with a design of monsters on it and worked all over with foliage." This piece alone amounted to 3,800 Spanish pesos. Also, still unsure of his guests' divine origin, Montezuma hosted them grandly with banquets and tours around the city. Cortés understood that he had finally found his lifelong dream of treasure, and he would do anything he needed to secure it. Therefore, in return for his hospitality, Montezuma was rewarded by being captured by Cortés.

The capture of Montezuma is symbolic in many ways, as it heralds the oppression and subversion of the Indian population to the new Spanish rulers. The emperor was held hostage in his own palace for eight months; later, when his citizens rebelled against the situation, Montezuma was forced by Cortés to appeal to them to be calm, but he was injured in the protest and died.

His successor, Cuauhtémoc, was more fierce in resisting Spanish rule. He led a battle against the Spanish conquistadors, throwing them out of Tenochtitlán and killing many of Cortés's men. However, Cortés fled and began plotting with other tribes who despised the Aztecs. In 1521, he, along with new allies, led a fresh assault on Tenochtitlán and captured Cuauhtémoc. Part of the strategy in defeating the Aztecs was to introduce diseases like smallpox, against which the Indians had no immunity; it killed scores of Indians, and their capital was finally captured— and razed to the ground—by Cortés and his men.

The sheer brutality of Cortés and his soldiers is quite possibly one of the reasons why, with only a few hundred men and some horses, he was able to conquer a great empire like the Aztecs. Before long, Mexico's millions of Indian natives were citizens of the newest colony of the Spanish crown, which took its name—Mexico—from the Aztec term the tribe used to refer to itself. Tenochtitlán, its glorious capital, would become Mexico City, the capital of an entirely new kind of nation.

CHAPTER

3

The
New Spain

ONE OF THE MOST IMPORTANT ASPECTS OF THE SPANISH CONQUEST OF Mexico is the fact that it was not only a conquest for financial reasons, but also for religious reasons. Those who accompanied Cortés on his expedition sought fortune, but they also wanted to glorify God in their mission. At the time of the conquest, which was complete by 1521, Spain as a nation was radically Catholic, having imposed the violent Inquisition to execute any Muslims or Jews who would not convert. King Charles V was approved by the pope in Rome to hold the responsibility of upholding Christianity in all of Spain's land holdings, including those in the New World.

At the time of the conquest, according to Lynn Foster, Spain had less than 8 million people. Mexico, most of which was under Aztec rule, contained approximately 25 million people. The thought of so many millions of unbaptized souls triggered a debate about how best to go about redeeming

32

these non-Christians, or "pagans," as the Spaniards considered them. The decision was made to begin to convert them to Catholicism.

The Spaniards set about this mission in multiple ways and from several directions. The first approach was the route adopted by Catholic friars, who began to immigrate to Mexico once they realized there was a mission of conversion there. Cortés had recommended that friars from the Dominican, Franciscan, and Augustinian orders—all of whom embraced humility and poverty as their lifestyles—be charged with converting Indian souls. Indeed, it was a good idea, as the local population admired these humble priests. Foster said, "They quickly impressed the native population by walking barefoot from the Gulf coast port to Mexico City. Their simple dress and self-inflicted suffering endured on their 50-day journey could not have contrasted more with the greed of the conquistadores." These friars sought souls, not gold.

By 1537, more than a decade after the friars first began arriving in Mexico, millions had been converted, often in mass baptisms, thousands at a time. Churches were constructed using the simple materials available in each region, since they had to be constructed quickly. The friars did not care to replicate the grand cathedrals that spotted the European landscape; simple, accessible chapels began cropping up all over Mexico. As the churches grew and the number of baptized souls increased, the Catholic Church as an institution in Mexico became more deeply entrenched—a legacy that remains to this day.

Alongside the churches grew local governments. Government officials were not as moral as the friars in their dealings with the native inhabitants. The concept of the *encomienda* was developed. The encomienda was a form of slave labor. Typically, the local natives who inhabited the land designated as the encomienda became the property—the slaves—of the landowner as well. They were simply considered part of the property, there to work the land. The Indians suffered

THEY BELIEVED THAT THEIR REWARD IN HEAVEN WOULD JUSTIFY ALL THEIR SUFFERINGS ON EARTH.

tremendously, being ripped away from their way of life and customs, and made to work long hours for little or no pay. Here, their newfound Catholic faith helped them make sense of their world: the faith centered on the beatitude, "The meek shall inherit the earth," and on a god who died on a cross in a brutal manner. What were their sufferings compared to his? They believed that their reward in heaven would justify all their sufferings on earth. The focus for them became the afterlife, not the cruelty of the present one.

It is important to note that not all Indians converted to Christianity; some converted just to save their livelihoods and escape punishment, while still practicing their own faith in private. Some created a Christian faith that was a combination or blend of their old faith with new Christian elements. Still others in some pockets of the region, especially in the south of Mexico, retained their old faith completely and rejected Christianity; they held on to their Indian languages, faith, and customs, although most of Mexico's central region became Spaniardized. Later in history, these pockets of resistance would rise up and reclaim their Indian heritage.

POVERTY IN NEW SPAIN

Mexico was referred to as New Spain, for good reason. Spaniards who wanted to start a new life and seek fortune, but could not do so in Spain—former criminals, bankrupt aristocrats, and others—flocked to the new land to establish themselves. There, they could live a good life cheaply, and they could also be of service to the crown, which needed to populate this expansive colony. In Spain, they had little promise of a future, but here they could be governors, mayors, landowners, and wealthy men. They could establish legacies of their own.

These Spanish immigrants, called *peninsulares* because they were born on the peninsula of Spain, arrived and re-created Spanish society, complete with its customs and traditions, as best as they could, to feel as "at home" as possible. They dressed in the Spanish and European fashions of the day, spoke in Spanish, and built homes in the colonial Spanish style.

The next generation born in Mexico were referred to as Creoles, and these were people of Spanish blood, the children of immigrants who did not have aristocratic origins. Then there were the *mestizos*, the Mexicans of mixed blood. As the colony developed, some Spaniards, especially the Creoles, intermarried or had children with the local Indians. Their children often had brown skin, not the white skin of the Spaniards. Still, these mestizos, who would eventually make up the majority of the Mexican population, enjoyed more privileges and rights than the Indians, who lived in distressing poverty.

Poverty went hand in hand with illiteracy. For its part, the church in Mexico embarked on a mission to educate the people it converted. The Dominican, Franciscan, and Augustinian friars believed in improving the lot of the people whom they converted, and education was part of this mission. In fact, the University of Mexico—the first university on the American continent—was established in 1551. Nevertheless, while illiteracy improved slowly, other conditions conspired to keep a class system—between wealthy peninsulares and Creoles on one side and mestizos and Indians on the other—firmly entrenched.

While the mestizos had a better chance of living well, life for the poor (most of whom were Indians) was incredibly difficult. The former system of the encomienda, in which entire towns and villages were "given" to a nobleman, had been outlawed by Charles V for many reasons, partly including the fact that it enslaved Indians. By 1542, the Catholic Church and the Spanish crown had decided that Indians were human

De Eſpañol, y Meſtiſa; Caſtiſa

Children of mixed parentage were referred to as mestizos, and many were able to receive proper schooling because of their Spanish heritage. Some children were sent back to Spain for their education, but most mestizos were tutored by traveling clergy.

beings and worthy of salvation. Therefore, they could not be enslaved. (To solve this problem, African slaves were imported to do the work.)

The outlawing of Indian slavery did not mean that they were treated well; instead they continued to be exploited by the hacienderos on whose land they worked. If they had a problem, few laws were in place to correct any injustices done to them. Furthermore, they suffered from disease—left untreated—and physical mistreatment.

Little was done to alleviate the suffering of the poor. The rates are startling. According to Foster, "At least one half of Indian children died in their first year; 75 percent died in early infancy. Excluded from formal education, their lot became that of illiterate and abjectly poor laborers and peasants." The problem of poverty, especially among Indians, is an issue that continues to plague Mexico today. Its roots are here, in the colonial subjection of the country.

THE GOVERNMENT OF COLONIAL MEXICO

The system of government on the haciendas reflected the way government in the colony was structured overall. In Spain, the Council of the Indies oversaw all laws and issues that arose in the colonies, including in Mexico. It was a "top-down" administration, in which the Spanish crown was the ultimate authority, although local officials in the colonies often wielded their own power for their own personal benefit.

The center of power was in the capital city, Mexico City. The wealthy and upper-class peninsulares and Creoles lived in the city, where everything from food to clothing to entertainment was available, while the poor lived on the fringes of the city. The viceroy—the monarch's representative in the colony—also resided in Mexico City, as did the heads of the Catholic Church. As in Spain, the monarch ruled in close contact with the church, which exerted considerable influence in governmental affairs.

Mexico City, however, was located in Mexico's central region, which was different from other areas of the new colony. In more far-flung areas, small colonial towns existed, usually established by the early friars in their explorations. In these towns, which served as the backdrop to many later American "cowboy" movies, the authority was the local *corregidore*, or administrator, who reported to the viceroy in Mexico City. However, the corregidores were often corrupt. Foster explained, they were "poorly paid and had limited authority, but they were notorious for finding ways to supplement their salaries. They oversaw and reported to the viceroy on the happenings in the municipality as well as in Indian settlements."

Of course, haciendas, whether they were located in a particular region of a town or not, were under the authority and governorship of their individual owners.

In some regions where there were not enough priests, haciendaeros, or Spanish officials to govern an area in which the vast majority were Indians, the system of caciques was created. The cacique, a governor of native Indian origin, was charged with overseeing "the indigenous peoples and fulfill[ing] Spanish tribute and tax levies," according to Foster.

THE CREOLE REVOLUTION

The class of Creoles became agitated. Though they had financially benefited from Mexico, they did not like the continued domination and dictatorship from across the ocean. They generally supported the Spanish monarchy, but they also wanted more say over governing themselves. They desired more independence, probably influenced by the revolutions in the United States and in France.

They had also started to think of themselves as "American," rather than as Spanish. They recognized their mixed heritage, and they adopted certain aspects of Indian culture, such as some of the language, cooking, and décor. They also began to criticize the brutality of the Spanish in their conquest of

Mexico and the lack of concern for the desperately poor in the colonies.

It was the reign of Charles IV of Spain (1788–1808) that tipped the scales in favor of revolution. The new king spent unwisely and paid off his country's debts by raiding the coffers of the colonies. Mexico was financially devastated when he did this, and the church was especially hard-hit because it could no longer continue its charitable works. Many Creoles were also financially affected, and as Foster said, "By mid-1810, Creoles in every major city had formed secret societies in opposition to the government."

One such Creole was Miguel Hidalgo, considered the father of Mexico. A priest, he witnessed firsthand the sufferings of the poor and the disdain of the Spanish monarchy for the welfare of its most vulnerable citizens. He was part of the Mexican Committee of Correspondence, an underground society that planned a rebellion. That rebellion was launched on September 16, 1810, and it adopted the Virgin of Guadalupe as its patron saint of sorts. The rebels confiscated land from the peninsulares and declared an end to the systems of slavery and heavy taxes. The rebellion, led by approximately 100,000 mostly poor people, became ferocious, as peninsulares and their families were killed mercilessly. Entire towns were seized by the rebels, until they dominated most of central Mexico. The rebellion was soon extinguished by forces loyal to the Spanish crown, and Hidalgo was captured and executed in 1811.

Another leader, Jose Maria Morelos, continued the banner of independence. He organized and trained small bands of fighters, whose priority was ending Spanish rule and establishing a free, unified Mexican nation that promised equality to all. They also adopted the Virgin of Guadalupe as their patron and fought bravely until they controlled most of the area around Mexico City. However, Morelos was himself captured in 1815 and executed by Spanish loyalists who were determined to end

In 1810, Father Hidalgo led the poor and oppressed people of the region to form a rebellion *(above)*. A Creole himself, Hidalgo found support with the mestizos and the enslaved Indians of the region in the fight for independence. Because of his efforts and sacrifice, September 16 is Independence Day in Mexico.

any ideas of insurrection, which threatened their high status and financial welfare.

The third and final attempt at independence came in 1821, when the Creoles, much more organized this time, agreed on a plan to unify all the rebellious groups who sought independence. Their plan, signed in February of 1821, was called the Plan of Iguala, and, according to Terri Dickinson on the Historical Text Archive Web site, it is also known as "the Plan of Three Guarantees as its main provisions were for independence, union with equality, and religion. The new nation of Mexico would be independent of Spain but maintain a constitutional monarchy that would be headed by King Ferdinand VII or another member of the royal family. The people of Mexico would be united through equality to all races. The national religion would be Roman Catholic and the Church would retain its privileged position."

The plan would be put into action via a military coup. Their leader, Agustín de Iturbide, seized Mexico City on September 27 later that same year.

A TRYING HALF-CENTURY

Although independence for Mexico had been achieved—at a great personal loss to the young nation—there were five difficult decades ahead, during which its ideals would be tested repeatedly.

Lynn Foster summarized the problem: "In its first 40 years, Mexico had more than 50 governments. . . . One year," she added, "there were as many as five changes in the presidency." To add to the turmoil, the United States, which was a relatively young nation itself, proved itself to be an unfriendly neighbor to the north.

Perhaps General Antonio López Santa Anna is the most infamous figure of Mexico during these initial decades of upset and chaos. A military leader, he was elected president in 1833, and he would serve in this position eleven times.

[Santa Anna] Spent Wastefully and Lived Lavishly, Making Decisions That Benefited Him Personally, Rather Than the Citizens of Mexico

In 1834, when his vice president put unpopular actions into effect, Santa Anna marched against him, suspended the constitution, and became a dictator. He spent wastefully and lived lavishly, making decisions that benefited him personally, rather than the citizens of Mexico, who suffered more than ever from poverty and neglect.

Mexico also suffered in terms of land loss under Santa Anna. In 1835, he led his army against a group of white U.S. citizens who had settled in northern Mexico (modern-day Texas) and wanted to secede from Mexico. These Anglo rebels, who included legends like Davy Crockett, holed themselves up in the Alamo, an old church, and resisted Santa Anna's forces, despite a long siege (which lent itself to the modern American adage, "Remember the Alamo!"). However, led by Sam Houston, the Anglos fought back and captured Santa Anna in a later battle, and to secure his freedom, Santa Anna signed away all the land north of the Rio Grande River, which constituted Texas.

The United States (which annexed Texas and much more land farther southwest) and Mexico erupted in war in 1846, declared by American president James K. Polk. Polk claimed that Mexico had encroached upon U.S. territory when it defended itself in a segment of its northern territory that the United States claimed as its own. The war lasted two years and resulted in the defeat of Mexico with the U.S. invasion of its capital in early 1848. The end was devastating for Mexico: it signed away most of its northern territories—half of its land— and was compensated a mere $18 million by the United States, which was, Foster said, "Less than half its annual budget."

The psychological impact of the loss was most devastating of all. According to Robert Ryal Miller on PBS.org, "The most lasting effect of the war on Mexicans was psychological. A tragic loss of soldiers and battles, the humiliation of having their capital and much of the country occupied by enemy troops, and the ignominy of a peace treaty that alienated half of the national territory (counting Texas) was a severe blow. It shattered a sense of national honor and dignity, and it engendered a deep and long-lasting feeling of resentment toward Yankees."

More loss was in Mexico's future, thanks to the corruption of its leaders, especially Santa Anna. Back in office, he continued to exploit the nation's already-crippled finances for his own benefit. In 1853, he sold 30,000 of northern Mexico (modern-day Arizona and New Mexico) to the United States to finance his lifestyle. Called the Gadsden Purchase, it was a tremendous boon to the expanding United States, but a huge loss to Mexico. It ended Santa Anna's political career.

It also cemented the outrage of Mexicans toward their northern neighbor, who they viewed as a land-grabbing, expansionist power. They also could not help but to view the contrast between their two nations: Mexico struggled with a corrupt and unstable government, a low literacy rate, and an inability to take advantage of industrial trends such as building railroads, whereas the United States reigned in these areas.

The distrust largely remains today, despite a lapse of more than 150 years.

4

An Age of Revolution(s)

A NEW GOVERNMENT ASSUMED POWER IN 1854, SWEPT IN BY THE Revolution of Ayutla, and it believed in, as Foster said, "free and honest elections, free public education, the separation of church and state, and a federalist republic" as outlined in the Mexican constitution.

Under leader Benito Juárez, an Indian, new reforms adhering to these ideals were instituted. Juárez is a beloved Mexican national figure, remembered for his solidarity with the poor and disenfranchised. Part of the revolution that finally overthrew Santa Anna, Juárez promised a new social order and stability for Mexico, based on the ideals of justice and equality. He was first elected in 1858, shortly after the new Mexican constitution of 1857 was adopted. He sought to uphold this constitution and bring order and stability to the nation. Indeed, as Foster said, "Under Benito Juárez, Mexico finally experienced a period of extended political stability and peace."

The constitution was not acceptable to all, however. For example, the Catholic Church, which had been an institution that wielded much power throughout Mexican history, was crippled by the new constitution. Under the new constitution, the church was not permitted to buy land or property for the purpose of generating income, and members of the clergy were banned from public office. All special privileges that clergy members had previously enjoyed were now suspended. The document established freedom of the press and education, which obstructed the church's involvement and ability to censor information, and it also established the right of the government to intervene in matters of worship. The new constitution was so controversial, in fact, that the pope denounced it.

In 1859, Juárez instituted the Reform Laws, which were an even more aggressive attack on the powers of the church. Under the Reform Laws, the government could (and did) seize all the properties of the church and sold many of them. Some say that the sale of these properties solved many financial problems for Mexico, as a testament to how much real estate the church actually possessed. The Reform Laws also took the government's power further, establishing civil marriage, as yet another step in separating church and state.

For this reason and others, President Juárez encountered several obstacles during his administration. In addition to the resistance many showed toward the new constitution, Juárez also had to deal with many threats against the nation, including the French invasion of Mexico. France attempted to impose a French-friendly monarchy in Mexico, but Juárez regained political ground and won reelection in 1867. "In the struggle to put down chronic political and social violence in the aftermath of the French intervention, Juárez sought to draw liberals and conservatives together in some sort of political consensus, although some accused him of running a dictatorship," wrote Roderic Camp and Colin MacLachlan.

President Benito Pablo Juarez *(above)* managed to create progress in a struggling nation when he took office after General Antonio López de Santa Anna's rule. Juarez, who was also busy defending Mexico against the imperialism of France, laid a strong foundation for future generations to build their nation.

By the time he died of a heart attack while in office in 1872, Juárez had overseen major improvements in Mexico, including reformation of many laws, the building of a railroad system to improve transportation, the building of primary schools, the establishment of a trained police force, and a slight boom to the economy. His successor, Sebastián Lerdo de Tejada, saw to it that Mexico was secularized even more, with the complete secularization of public education.

PORFIRIO DIAZ

In 1876, Porfirio Diaz became president of Mexico. His presidency, which lasted until 1910, ushered Mexico into the new century, but it also established a legacy of corruption and distrust in Mexican politics. Historian Brian Hamnett wrote in *A Concise History of Mexico* that between 1884 to the end of his reign in 1910, "Diaz consolidated his personal rule" in Mexico. Lynn Foster explained that, "Because all he achieved was at the expense of the Mexican people, he is considered the villain in 20th-century Mexican history." The era of his rule is referred to as the "Porfiriato."

When he first came to power, Porfirio Diaz was quite popular. He was a mestizo who had made his career in the army and served in Congress during Juárez's presidency. He attempted to run for the presidency, but lost, and so led a revolt against the government, which he toppled in 1876. His slogan was "no reelection," which was an idea that attracted those who had become disillusioned by Juárez's four terms in office. To have a president who could serve only one term meant greater democracy and an end to a president who could become a lifelong dictator.

However, Diaz soon proved to be as power-hungry as any against whom he railed. When his first term as president technically ended in 1880, he had someone stand in as a candidate, thereby bypassing the constitution of 1857 and his own "no reelection" dictum.

As a leader, Diaz was tough—especially on his own people. He did not tolerate political dissent and ensured "peace" through fear. He expanded the police force, which ruthlessly suppressed Mexican citizens who protested his actions, and any demonstrations by Indians or the poor against corruption were broken up violently. People could be arrested for anything that was interpreted as disturbing the social order.

While people's civil rights were certainly violated during the Porfiriato, it can be said that social order was achieved. Crime rates decreased, even as political frustration increased. Diaz also worked closely with the church, supporting its ability to operate almost independently of the government and not enforcing limits on its power.

Diaz also had the support of the middle class and the wealthy Creoles in Mexico because he did, in the end, modernize Mexico more than any leader before him, which boosted the nation's economy and status on the world scene. Because Mexico was more "orderly," without governmental upsets and frequent uprisings, it was stable, and foreign countries felt more comfortable investing in it. In fact, as Foster said, "With domestic peace and a sensible budget, Mexico was deemed one of the most creditworthy nations in the world" during the Porfiriato. Foreign trade "increased nearly tenfold" during this era, she added, and the railroad system was expanded, so that by the end of the Porfiriato, a rail network of over 15,000 had been built and was being actively used for personal transportation as well as commerce. The railroad system, of course, was a major factor in Mexico's increased ability to expand and strengthen its economy.

The Porfiriato, at the time, was seen as one of the greatest eras of progress in Mexican history. Of course, now, a century later, historians agree that such progress came at the expense of the majority of the Mexican people—the poor—while it benefited the wealthy and middle classes. Still, a new sense of Mexican identity developed during this time period, and the arts and culture flourished. Educational opportunities were expanded, most notably for women, who trained to be teachers, for example. There were two Mexicos, however: Though the number of schools expanded and the middle and upper classes became more professionalized, the national illiteracy rate was an astonishing 80 percent. The progress of the Porfiriato did not reach the poor rural areas and the southern part of Mexico, where some of the greatest poverty existed.

In fact, by the end of Porfirio Diaz's rule, only 2 percent of the Mexican population were landowners, according to Foster. Many Indians saw their land confiscated, and thus entire families were dispossessed of their properties. The poor often sold themselves to work off their debt, thus ensuring that generations of their families would suffer in this way, unable to rise above their social class.

Diaz had also been very friendly to the Catholic Church, which had slowly begun to reacquire its power and rebuild its wealth under his rule.

The class system was more racist than ever under Diaz. As their sense of pride in their Mexican heritage blossomed, many middle- and upper-class Mexicans, who were doing well financially, came to view the poor Indian population as backwards and uncivilized. They did not see a connection between the way the government had treated the Indians since 1521 and the current squalor in which many tribes existed. Uprisings were suppressed brutally because they were seen as a threat to the well-being of these upper classes. In fact, many came to believe that the Indians had fallen into such a terrible state because they themselves lacked the innovation and work ethic to improve their lives. Such racism only grew more entrenched as the years under Diaz's rule continued.

THE REVOLUTION OF 1910

Two Mexicos existed by 1910, the last year of the Porfiriato. One Mexico belonged to the small middle and upper class, which was literate, educated, wealthy, and land-owning. The other Mexico belonged to the majority of Mexicans: the poor, mostly Indian, peasants, many of whom were homeless, most of whom were unemployed and illiterate. While Europe and the United States smiled at the progress Mexico was making under Diaz, they did not see—because Diaz's government kept it hidden—the terrible conditions of the poor, including the lack of voice in government, the high mortality rate, and the lack of hope for a better future.

Like most dictatorships, Diaz's came to an end because he eventually managed to make enough citizens unhappy with the current state of affairs. Between 1907 and 1908, the economy fell into a depression; thus, many of the middle and upper classes who supported him because his policies financially benefited them began to itch for change. The poor, who had always despised Diaz, were also ready to revolt, having been frustrated for more than thirty years by his brutal and suppressive policies.

On November 20, 1910—two months after Mexico celebrated a century of independence from Spanish rule—civil war erupted. Small bands of rebels, who were uncoordinated but fueled by frustration and need for radical change, revolted against Diaz and his dictatorial regime. Some of the heroes of the Mexican revolution included Francisco Madero, Emiliano Zapata, and Pancho Villa—local rebels who helped organize and perpetuate the revolution. Though Diaz fought the rebels, his army was eventually overcome and surrendered on May 21, 1911.

The civil war did not end with Diaz's defeat; in fact, the leaders who succeeded Diaz, such as Madero and Victoriano Huerta, met with obstacles and continued fighting. The government of Mexico was unstable once again, with rivaling factions striving to solidify their power and control of the nation. The ones who suffered the most, of course, were Mexican civilians, who were caught in the cross fire. Before the Mexican Revolution was over, nearly two million people had died.

Pancho Villa *(center, left)* and Emiliano Zapata *(center, right)* pose for pictures in the Presidential Palace, backed by faithful soldiers. From humble beginnings, these two rebels rose to become revolutionary leaders who toppled Mexico's ineffective government. The quote, "It is better to die on your feet than live on your knees," is often attributed to Zapata.

Venustiano Carranza and his Constitutional Army of the North seized control of the government in 1916, with the help of the United States (which interfered in Mexican politics—not for the first time—to protect its business interests). He did little to solve the chaos of the revolution and even less to restore order; in fact, he ordered the assassination of Emiliano Zapata, who was very popular among the poor and peasant classes, in 1919, and killed thousands of his followers, known as Zapatistas, before they succeeded. However, Carranza

PUBLIC WORSHIP OUTSIDE OF CHURCH BUILDINGS WAS OUTLAWED.

is responsible for helping to usher in the new constitution, although he was not happy with the results.

In December of 1916, Carranza held a session of 200 delegates and charged them with hammering out a constitution. He hoped they would slightly rework and legitimize a new version of the 1857 constitution, but instead they made more sweeping changes. The new constitution included major social reforms, such as eliminating debt peonage and establishing protections for workers. It redistributed land to the poor and put limits on estates of the wealthy.

The constitution of 1917 also restricted the powers of the Catholic Church, which had enjoyed a period of growth under Porfirio Diaz. The new constitution resembled the previous constitution, which had been upheld by Benito Juárez, in its limits on the role the church could play in Mexican politics and society. For example, secular education in Mexican schools would be enforced, according to the new constitution. Public worship outside of church buildings was outlawed. Even more severe were the provisions that banned monastic orders and the right of the church to own or administer property. Also, church property that served the public, such as schools and hospitals, was nationalized, or taken over by the government. The line between church and state was defined more clearly than ever.

The new constitution also protected Mexico's natural resources and limited the powers of foreign investors and corporations. It also emphasized the "no reelection" policy for the presidency.

As Foster said, "For the first time the social concerns of most Mexicans and most revolutionaries were formulated. Institutions that had crippled the state in the past were weakened: the church, foreign interests, and haciendas."

The 1917 constitution included many important reforms, which looked appealing on paper. However, it was up to the new government to now enforce this new constitution. Carranza did not meet this challenge. Instead, he continued to try to consolidate his power and disregarded most of the reforms called for in the new constitution. His 1919 assassination of Emiliano Zapata only fueled more anger and frustration toward his administration.

Álvaro Obregón, the minister of war, and other regional leaders finally chased Carranza out of office. He was executed in 1920, which marked the end of the devastating Mexican Revolution.

Finally, Mexico was about to embark on another period of relative stability.

THE RESTORATION OF PEACE

Obregón can be credited with restoring peace to Mexico, and he did so mainly by being inclusive. He invited people from the different political factions and revolutionary groups to serve in government positions, thus offering them a voice in his new administration. This placated most of them and encouraged a spirit of cooperation, which was much needed after 10 years of a crippling and destabilizing civil war.

Committed to land reform and solving the problem of poverty, Obregón redistributed land to Indians and the poor, thus adhering to the reforms mandated by the 1917 constitution. Though he was a capitalist, knowing that business would strengthen the economy, he also supported the rights of workers, especially their rights to organize into unions. He also encouraged education and was committed to lowering the illiteracy rate, and he had much success in these areas.

In other areas, Obregón was weak. Though he agreed in theory with the anti-church provisions of the constitution, he did not enforce the majority of them. Later, when the church criticized the government, those reforms were put into effect and the church found its powers severely restricted. Also, he was not able to stand up to the United States, which put pressure on his government to allow it to maintain its business interests, though they contradicted the constitution's mandate that Mexico own its own natural resources. For these things, Obregón's presidency ended on a sour note, despite its promising beginning.

Plutarco Elías Calles was president of Mexico from 1924 until 1928, and he instituted a constitutional change that allowed for nonconsecutive reelection. In other words, a president could be reelected, but not immediately after his first term. Therefore, Obregón ran again for office in 1928 and won a second term, despite an election that was contested and controversial. On July 17, 1928, however, he was assassinated by a faction loyal to the church, known as the Cristeros, who opposed the government's policies against the Catholic Church, according to Foster.

CHAPTER
5
Calderón and the New Politics

PLUTARCO ELÍAS CALLES REMAINED IN OFFICE AFTER OBREGÓN'S assassination, and Mexico entered an era known as the Maximato, after Calles, who referred to himself as the Jefe Máximo (or political chief). Calles left an important legacy: the Partido Nacional Revolucionario, or the National Revolutionary Party (PNR), to which he assigned much political power. Later, it would become the Partido Revolucionario Institucional, or the Institutional Revolutionary Party (PRI). Calles adhered to the "no reelection" policy, but he ruled from behind a string of puppet presidents who all belonged to the PRI, thus ensuring that the PRI vision of Mexican politics endured.

Lázaro Cárdenas was the exception to the rule of Calles's puppet presidents. When he assumed power in 1934 (thanks to Calles's help), Cárdenas did not allow the Jefe Máximo to dictate his policies. He considered himself a president of the people, and he campaigned to seek support from all over

Mexico, not just the more prosperous central region. He redistributed more land than anyone else, finally ending the system of the hacienda and putting more land than ever in the hands of the poor.

Cárdenas's greatest success was probably the nationalization of oil. In the past, Mexican oil had been an important part of its economy, and Mexico provided many foreign countries with oil. However, as a natural resource, oil was controlled by foreign companies, to the detriment of the average Mexican citizen who saw profits from oil production mostly flow out of the country. Cárdenas settled the issue once and for all: In 1938, he seized the holdings of 17 British and U.S. oil companies, offering $10 million for them in compensation. The amount was renegotiated by the outraged corporations, who demanded much more, but settled for $24 million. Mexicans saw this as an issue of national pride, and Cárdenas was a hero for restoring Mexican dignity. In 1940, he resigned peacefully from the presidency, according to the "no reelection" policy and mandate of the constitution.

A CLOSED OR OPEN GOVERNMENT?

The PRI had now been in power successively since 1930, and its candidates for every presidential election easily won every time. Corruption was rampant. Many of its officials grew their own wealth as a result of their political positions. Local officials—from police chiefs to bureaucrats—required bribes to perform the simplest tasks on behalf of the citizens, and the average person became frustrated to see those with political responsibility live luxurious lifestyles, while the majority of the population lived in squalor.

The PRI also elected presidents who ruled with a heavy hand. President Gustave Díaz Ordaz was elected in 1964, and his attitude toward dissent was to quell it as quickly as possible. In 1968, a public fight between students was broken up brutally by the police force in Mexico City, causing many students

[PRESIDENT ORDAZ] WAS THE ONE WHO ORDERED THE SNIPERS TO SHOOT DOWN INTO THE CROWD.

and others to protest the treatment of the youth at the hands of the paramilitary force. Over the next few months, students led marches and demonstrations, leading many of them to be imprisoned unfairly and without cause.

The unrest finally culminated in a horrific massacre, known as the Tlatelolco Massacre. On October 2, 1968, a large demonstration in a public square, the Plaza de las Tres Culturas in Tlatelolco, a neighborhood of Mexico City, was violently dissembled in one of the greatest controversies in Mexican history. Though the protest was peaceful, snipers shot down into the crowds, triggering the police to shoot at the protestors. The number who died is disputed but probably ranges in the hundreds.

The awful facts, revealed later, after Ordaz's death in 1979, showed that President Ordaz —nervous because he feared that the demonstrations of the past few months would threaten the 1968 Olympics, which Mexico was sponsoring—had government agents planted as snipers in the apartment building above the plaza, and that he was the one who ordered the snipers to shoot down into the crowd. He did this so that he would be justified in having the police use violence against the protestors to break up the rally. He also hoped that, by implying that the rally was a violent one, public support of the months of protests would wane.

As Foster said, "The PRI never recovered from the tragedy at Tlatelolco." However, the PRI seemed not to understand the damage it had sustained, since its next candidate for president was Luis Echeverría Alvarez, who had been Ordaz's interior minister and was implicated in the responsibility for orchestrating the massacre. Ronald Ecker, author of "The Tlatelolco Massacre in Mexico," wrote, "Any hopes that the trauma of

Protestors gathered in the Tlatelolco Square in Mexico City two days before the 1968 Olympics, hoping that international attention would influence the Mexican government into giving them more decisive power in politics. The authorities, however, overreacted to the demonstration, and brutally and forcefully ended the peaceful protest with gunfire.

Tlatelolco might lead to some conciliatory move, some trend toward political reform, with the choice of Díaz Ordaz's successor were dashed when the PRI's choice for the 1970 presidential election turned out to be Luis Echeverría Álvarez. As Díaz Ordaz's interior minister, Echeverría was in charge of internal security at the time of the Tlatelolco Massacre, and was widely suspected of complicity in the killings if not actually ordering them."

Indeed, Echeverría Alvarez went on to be involved in other brutal suppressions of human rights, including the Corpus Christi Massacre in 1971, in which at least 25 students were killed during a protest by another faction of the police force in Mexico City. The PRI, which had done much good for the benefit of Mexico in the earlier part of the century, was now seen as public enemy number one by the Mexican people.

RIFT WITH THE CHURCH

When the Spaniards conquered Mexico in 1521, they set about almost immediately on the project of converting the 25 million people they now governed. Since that time, the Catholic Church in Mexico has played a pivotal role in Mexican society, politics, and even the economy. In the past few decades, the church has struggled, especially under the dominance of the PRI and the growth of other churches (the constitution of Mexico in 1917 permitted freedom of religion so that the Catholic Church did not have a monopoly on souls).

Mary Jordan of the *Washington Post* wrote, "The Roman Catholic Church continues to be so influential in Mexico that it rivals the federal government for impact on people's lives, yet in many corners of the country, it is fast losing ground to Protestant churches." Indeed, the Catholic Church in Mexico feels a threat to its place: The Protestant churches and more evangelical movements have grown in their influence and size. Furthermore, more and more Mexicans believe that the church does not have a place in their lives whatsoever. "In a country where nearly every town has been centered on a Roman Catholic church since the Spanish conquistadors arrived 500 years ago and imposed Catholicism, the rising number of church defectors is seen as a wake-up call for the Rome-based

Despite the Roman Catholic Church's initial presence in Mexico, other Christian-based religions are gaining popularity in rural areas. Organizations such as Light of the World Church were founded in Guadalajara City in 1926, and have more than 5 million members all over the world. Here, Light of the World church leader Samuel Joaquin Flores greets his followers from a balcony during a celebration in 2005.

church to become more available and relevant to people," added Jordan.

The church also struggles to regain an official role in Mexico's political system, since the many decades of PRI rule have been unfriendly. In the past, as more people grew dissatisfied with the PRI, however, a sense that Mexico was growing too secular was also developing. That same feeling slowly aided in the rise of another political party in Mexico.

THE PAN RISES

After the Tlatelolco Massacre of 1968, many leaders in Mexican society left the PRI, such as the writer Octavio Paz and other intellectuals, as well as most of its youth base. Many people sought other parties, one of which was the Partido Acción Nacional, or the National Action Party (PAN).

The PAN was formed in 1939 by Roman Catholics and conservatives who rejected the way that the Catholic Church allowed the government to suppress citizens' rights; in exchange, the government allowed the church to exercise a certain amount of influence, even though it had technically been banned from intervening in politics since the Mexican Revolution. Over the years, facing the daunting PRI, the PAN nevertheless made small strides by winning local elections and even placing candidates in gubernatorial elections. As people grew disenchanted with the PRI, the PAN offered an interesting alternative: a Christian democracy that embraced neither left-wing nor right-wing ideologies. Rather the PAN advocated adopting a policy, whether liberal or conservative, that suited the problem at hand. It tended to support social conservative issues, however, because of its Catholic roots, as well as conservative positions, such as a smaller role for government and little regulation over business and the private sector.

As the PAN and other parties began forming and defining their political platforms, several issues became prominent. The issues included poverty, unemployment, overpopulation, the growing numbers of Mexicans crossing the northern border into the United States to seek work, and literacy. One of the most important issues—dear to many people—was open elections. After living through so many years of PRI rule, people felt that the elections should be scrutinized more closely. Others called for broader reform, aimed at making the Mexican government more open and democratic.

FELIPE CALDERÓN

Felipe de Jesús Calderón Hinojosa was born on August 18, 1962 in Morelia, in the Mexican state of Michoacán, the eldest son in a family of six boys and two girls. His parents, Luis Calderon and Maria del Carmen Hinojosa Gonzalez, sent him to Catholic schools and educated him about politics at an early age. In fact, when his schoolteacher asked his class what they wanted to be when they grew up, a young Calderón clearly replied, "presidente de la república."

People who know what Calderón's childhood was like would hardly be surprised. His father, Luis Calderón, an ethics teacher, was actually a co-founder of the PAN and was devoted to promoting its cause. He also served in a number of political and governmental positions on a state and federal level.

As a teenager, Luis Calderón grew up at the time of the Cristero Rebellion, which President Calles attempted to suppress. The Rebellion, sparked in 1927, was a reaction to the way in which the Mexican Constitution of 1917—and the way it was enforced by Calles—took power away from the Catholic Church. Specifically, the constitution banned religious schools, making all schools secular, and it also banned priests and clergy from wearing their religious vestments in public and from voting and taking part in political life. The rebels, who rose up when Calles began enforcing these constitutional provisions, called themselves "Cristeros," because they believed they were fighting for Jesus Christ himself.

A devout Catholic, Luis Calderón was caught up in the Rebellion. He had become disenchanted with the way the Church's role was being detached from that of the government and he did not think Mexico should become a totally secular society. He saw the removal of religion from public life as immoral and unrealistic, a point made more relevant when he was expelled from the state university for wearing a crucifix. Calderón sought ways to preserve a tie between public life and personal faith: this is what led him and others to establish the movement that would become the PAN.

GROWING UP IN THE PAN

A political activist, Luis Calderón also involved his young family in politics. Lacey wrote that Felipe Calderón's "first campaign, his family likes to say, came in 1962 when he was still in the womb. It was a governor's race in Michoacán State that his father . . . was managing. His pregnant mother was pitching in, as well." Lacey added, "There were other races, many others, all of them family affairs. Young Felipe handed out leaflets when other children were out playing ball. He rode around in a truck with loudspeakers when his contemporaries were hanging out in the park."

Felipe Calderón studied at the Escuela Libre de Derecho in Mexico City, where he earned his bachelor's degree in law, then went on to earn a master's degree in economics from the Instituto Tecnológico Autónomo de Mexico. When he was nineteen years old, he witnessed his father grow disillusioned with the PAN. Luis Calderón left the PAN in 1981 because he felt it had strayed from its mission and ideals.

The younger Calderón, however, continued to embrace the PAN's ideology. In 1987, he was the secretary of studies. He later earned a master's degree in public administration from Harvard University, and upon returning to Mexico, he dedicated much of his time to the PAN. He served as the party's national youth secretary in 1991 and then as secretary-general in 1993. While serving the PAN, he also established a professional career, putting his legal experience and studies to work at firms like Goodrich, Riquelme, and Partners and Multibanco Comermex.

Felipe Calderón *(right)* and his wife, Margarita Zavala *(left)*, both had fathers that were heavily involved in the National Action Party (PAN) in Mexico. Together, they have worked on PAN campaigns and Calderón's own presidential campaign, and have raised three children.

He served in local and national politics as a young man; he held positions in the legislative assembly and in the federal Chamber of Deputies. Calderón also continued to rise through the ranks of the PAN. At 34 years old, he was chairman of the party. He met his wife, Margarita Zavala, also a PAN supporter and congresswoman, and has three children with her. During Vicente Fox's administration, he served as director of Banobras, a national development bank, and as the secretary of energy.

He was raised a devout Roman Catholic and attended mass regularly with his family. His political and social views include opposition to abortion, euthanasia, and contraception, in line with the views of the church.

When he was nominated to be the PAN's candidate for president, he was only 44 years old, one of the youngest Mexican presidents.

6

Revamping Mexican Politics

WHEN PRESIDENT MIGUEL DE LA MADRID HURTADO WAS ELECTED IN 1982, he promised publicly to clean up corruption in Mexican politics and to deliver more honest elections. While he allowed the opposing party, PAN, to make electoral gains on a local level, he also turned a blind eye to the ejection of opposing candidates in gubernatorial elections. Furthermore, in his memoir, published in 2004, de la Madrid revealed that the presidential elections of 1988, in which his successor Carlos Salinas de Gortari was elected, were rigged. As the ballots were counted and it was clear that opposition candidate Cuauhtémoc Cárdenas, son of popular former president Lázaro Cárdenas, was winning, the PRI declared victory, stating that the computers storing ballot data had broken down. Obviously many protested, claiming that the breakdown of the computerized system was a convenient occurrence, but there was no way for challengers to demand a "recount." Later, the paper ballots were burned so that proof of the fraud would never be found. The PRI claimed victory in the election, claiming that Salinas de Gortari had won by a thin margin.

"The electoral upset was a political earthquake for us," de la Madrid wrote in his memoir, according to a *New York Times* article by Ginger Thompson. "As in any emergency, we had to act because the problems were rising fast. There was not a moment for great meditation, we needed agility in our response to consolidate the triumph of the PRI."

However, he had opened up the system slightly, and that wedge was all that the Mexican people needed to insert themselves and rally for reform.

As written by Foster, Salinas de Gortari himself said in 1988, "This is a historic time. Everyone's clamoring for more democracy." But it was becoming clear that the PRI was not the party to provide the Mexican people with what they wanted. It was too steeped in the ways of the past, the ways of corruption and personal gain.

UPRISINGS AND SCANDALS

President Salinas de Gortari, despite the fraudulent election that put him in office, tried hard to gain the support of the Mexican people. He enacted several policies that were popular, including allowing the political process to be more open (which helped win more support, ironically, for the PAN). His background in economics (he had a Ph.D. degree from Harvard University in political economics and government) and his previous experience as minister of the Bureau of Planning and Budget helped him to understand how to improve Mexico's dire economic situation.

Early in his presidency, he helped to stabilize the economy, and by 1991, it was even expanding at a promising rate. He encouraged and made foreign companies and corporations feel comfortable in choosing Mexico for investment. Salinas de Gortari also made sure that profits were turned into development projects, such as highways. People's lives became more convenient as technological advances made their way to Mexican cities. Modernization was at hand.

However, as Lynn Foster pointed out, not much was done to alleviate the contrast between the two Mexicos: the Mexico of modernity and the Mexico of poverty. Salinas de Gortari's presidency did little to help the poorest of Mexico's citizens, those who depended on the land and lived far from the urban areas.

The Zapatista uprising on January 1, 1994, awakened the world to the plight of Mexico's peasants. On that day, 2,000 armed Maya Indians rebelled against the government, demanding the right to their land and a stop to discrimination. The Ejército Zapatista de Liberación Nacional, or Zapatista National Liberation Army (EZLN), essentially declared war on the Mexican government, beginning with the takeover of five towns in the poor southern state of Chiapas, where they originated.

They are called Zapatistas because they follow the ideology of Emiliano Zapata. Zapata, one of the heroes of the Mexican Revolution of 1910, advocated *Tierra y Libertad*, or "land and liberty" as the way to "fix" Mexico's problems. From poor origins himself, Zapata strongly believed that the major issue facing Mexico was the mistreatment of its poorest citizens, who had been dispossessed of their land. He put forth the Plan de Ayala, which outlined a plan for restoring land seized by Porfirio Diaz's government from the poor, most of whom lived in Mexico's impoverished southern states. When a person owned land, Zapata believed, he could support himself; he could raise livestock and grow crops to sustain his family. This would solve, over time, the terrible problem of poverty in Mexico.

Mexican leaders since 1910 had neglected the poor, however, and Zapata's ideas were dismissed. During the New Year's Day Revolt in 1994, the Zapatistas listed their complaints and

Echoing the beliefs of Emiliano Zapata, Mayan Indians took up arms in the southern part of Mexico and called themselves Zapatistas *(above)*. Essentially declaring war on the national government, these guerillas battled soldiers in the jungles of Mexico before a new president, Vicente Fox, made efforts to establish peace. Fox put his own spin on a Zapatista saying and told the Indians of his country, "Never again a Mexico without you."

demands. A key point of their revolt was the protest of NAFTA, the North American Free Trade Agreement, which Mexico had signed and which went into effect that same day. NAFTA was a trade bloc among the United States, Canada, and Mexico. It essentially eliminated tariffs and investment restrictions on goods and products traded among the three member countries.

THE ARMY WENT INTO CIVILIAN AREAS AND KILLED MANY INNOCENT PEOPLE IN ORDER TO QUASH THE REBELS.

While businesses were set to benefit from NAFTA, poor farmers saw the price of their goods fall even farther.

The Zapatista uprising warned Mexicans that NAFTA was an assault on the livelihoods of poor farmers and peasants, who had been neglected for too long due to the racism against indigenous Indians. As one Zapatista fighter said, "We rose up in arms not so we could have somewhere—an office, or some other important place to go—We took up arms so we would not be killed by forgetfulness . . . so the demands would be heard and they would see that in this corner, in this country, Mexico, there are indigenous peoples who have been abandoned for many years," according to a Democracy Now transcript.

The uprising drew national and international attention to the plight of the poor in Mexico. In *Mexico: From Montezuma to the Fall of the PRI*, Jaime Suchlicki wrote, "According to foreign organizations such as the United Nations Food and Agriculture Organization (FAO), approximately 41 million Mexicans do not obtain adequate food. Of these, 17 million live in extreme poverty and suffer from malnutrition." Approximately 9 million people live in extreme poverty in the southern rural states of Chiapas, Oaxaca, Veracruz, and elsewhere; in these areas, Suchlicki added, "as many as 80 percent of the peasants are poor."

The brutal repression of the Zapatista uprising by the Mexican government also highlighted, more than ever, the need for democratic reform. The army went into civilian areas and killed many innocent people in order to quash the rebels, but the damage such actions did to the government's reputation was severe.

It was worsened by a scandal that tainted the reputation of Carlos Salinas de Gortari. Though he had done much to improve Mexico's economy (indeed, he had initiated NAFTA on Mexico's behalf), it was revealed later, during the presidency of President Ernesto Zedillo, that Salinas de Gortari had been corrupted in the worst of ways.

In 1994, PRI secretary-general José Francisco Ruiz Massieu was assassinated in Mexico City. Massieu had been Salinas de Gortari's brother-in-law, and his murder went unsolved until President Zedillo appointed a special investigator, in an attempt to shed the PRI's corrupt, secretive image. "Let it be clear," declared the new president. "Nobody can be above the law. In Mexico, impunity has ended," according to an article by Kevin Fedarko in *Time*. In 1995, the investigation led to the doorstep of Raul Salinas, former president Salinas de Gortari's older brother. Another person implicated was Mario Ruiz Massieu, the murdered man's brother and former attorney general, who allegedly tried to cover up details of his own brother's assassination. Ruiz Massieu fled the country as details of his cover-up emerged, and he was arrested at Newark Airport in New Jersey, carrying large amounts of money in his suitcase. It was later discovered that Raul Salinas had over $300 million stashed away in European banks, money he had made by profiting from his and his brother's political positions.

The connection between Carlos and Raul Salinas de Gortari and Mario Ruiz Massieu shocked Mexicans, especially as more details were clarified. Foster said, "Corruption was revealed to have touched everything, from the way tortillas are made to the sale of state-owned agencies, from protection of drug kingpins to murder." While Raul Salinas sat in jail, his brother Carlos's former reputation as the president who modernized Mexico was devastated; Carlos Salinas de Gortari fled Mexico and his legacy was forever connected to greed and corruption.

In 1996, Felipe Calderón became president of the PAN party. He was determined to expand the PAN's political gains so that the corruption of the PRI party could be stopped and a new alternative offered to the Mexican people.

THE ELECTION OF 2000

Though President Zedillo was viewed favorably by Mexicans for refusing to stop in the quest for truth in the Ruiz Massieu assassination, though it led to the former president's family, the reputation of the PRI was in shambles. The PAN, at the same time, was winning points for its conservative stance and pledge to be free of corruption. Jaime Suchlicki, author of *Mexico: From Montezuma to the Fall of the PRI*, wrote, "Official corruption; suspicions of party officials' involvement in political conspiracies, drugs, and assassinations; and the precipitous collapse in prestige of the hitherto popular former President Salinas all contributed to the PRI's reversal of fortunes." He added, "Groups hurt by past policies united against the PRI."

The elections of 2000 were a major turning point in Mexican history: As Mexico closed one century and began a new one, it seemed that things had to change. Mexico had to shed an old political party just as it shed an old century, filled with upheaval and corruption.

VICENTE FOX

The PAN put forth Vicente Fox Quesada as its presidential candidate. The tall, affable Fox was a perfect choice; Mexicans respected his business experience as an executive in the Coca-Cola company, and they loved his charming personality and intelligence. During his campaign, he promised to bring his business acumen to solve Mexico's fiscal problems, to reform Mexico's democracy, to protect human rights, to alleviate unemployment, and to begin new talks with the United States, to which more than 6 million Mexicans had already illegally fled to find work.

Suchlicki described Fox as "a successful entrepreneur with a social conscience" who "criticized the PRI for its 'seventy-one years of corruption, impotence, and poverty'"; he questioned whether Mexicans wanted change or another six years of PRI rule; he successfully courted the Catholic Church,

Offering an alternative choice to the Mexican public, the National Action Party (PAN) was created as a neutral party, one that didn't lean to left- or right- wing ideologies. Raised in a Roman Catholic family that was involved in PAN since its creation, Felipe Calderón is an ideal representative for the party and, many believe, of the Mexican public. *Above*, as president of PAN, Calderon meets with U.S. president Bill Clinton in 1997.

which the PRI had neglected; and he finally appealed to the masses with his open-necked shirt, blue jeans, cowboy boots and plain talking."

The PAN won 42.5 percent of the votes over the PRI's 36.1 percent. (A third party, the growing PRD, gained 16.6 percent.) Mexicans were thrilled to have finally shed the PRI's domination over their political system; it was a promising and hopeful time. Not only was it the first election that saw the victory of an opposition-party candidate, but it was the first election in Mexico in many decades that was considered open, honest, and fair.

During Vicente Fox's administration, Felipe Calderón, who was continuing his rise up through the ranks of the PAN party, served as director of Banobras, a national development bank, and later as Fox's Secretary of Energy. He worked hard at his post, although some insiders suggested that he did not always agree with Vicente Fox on issues.

Fox's first few years in office went well. According to Foster, since Fox's election, "Mexico has become a more open society and a less corrupt one. The press has never been freer—or more critical. . . . All branches of government, not just the executive, have become more independent and less secretive." Fox had ordered investigations into previous scandals, such as the Tlatelolco Massacre, allowing secret files to be opened for the first time. (Luis Echeverría Alvarez, former president of Mexico, was eventually arrested and charged with genocide for his involvement in that and the Corpus Christi Massacre.)

Fox seemed to initially deliver on his promise for change. However, his early presidency was marred by several events. His campaign promise to open negotiations about migrant workers with the United States came to a crashing halt after the United States suffered a terrorist attack on September 11, 2001, which killed approximately 3,000 people. This attack led Mexico's northern neighbor to guard its borders more carefully and cautiously than ever before. However, seeking work, Mexicans continued to cross the border. In fact, Brian Hamnett wrote, "In August 2005, the State Governors of New Mexico and Arizona declared a state of emergency along the

Mexican border, arguing that illegal immigration was out of control." Fox also lost favor with U.S. president George W. Bush, some speculate, when Mexico opposed the U.S. invasion of Iraq in 2003.

Also, while Fox had many ideas and presented many plans to Congress, the Congress—divided among various political factions—did not approve many of his plans. Hamnett wrote, "Fox's measures had been largely hindered by Congress. During the second half of his term, he seemed to have lost authority and direction altogether."

Furthermore, many Mexican factories and *maquiladoras* (Mexican plants that assemble imported raw material and sell them as exports for foreign businesses) lost work to new plants in other countries, such as China, which promised cheaper labor to companies. Jaime Suchlicki wrote about the importance of the United States to Mexico's economy: "The United States is Mexico's most important customer, accounting for 89.3 percent of Mexico's exports—including petroleum, automobiles, auto parts, and vegetables in 1999." However, some of these sales began to go elsewhere, to other countries that promised cheaper prices.

7

The Election of 2006

AS THE PRIMARY SEASON GOT UNDERWAY, FELIPE CALDERÓN RESIGNED from his post as Secretary of Energy to seek the nomination of the PAN for president. He was hurt to learn that President Vicente Fox supported someone else for the nomination. However, the primary polls across the country demonstrated that Calderón actually had more support than had previously been thought.

This support may have been due to his lifelong career working for the PAN in many different positions. Also, three of his four siblings all had political careers: For example, his sister Luisa served in the Michoacan legislature, in the Chamber of Deputies, and as a Senator. Juan Luis, their brother, was a federal deputy, and another sister Carmen de Fatima also worked in the federal government.

Four out of five of Luis Calderón's children had thus continued to work in the PAN, though the party, according to the elder Calderón, had long abandoned its Christian socialist

HE WAS HURT TO LEARN THAT PRESIDENT VICENTE FOX SUPPORTED SOMEONE ELSE FOR THE NOMINATION.

roots and become a party that catered to the interests of the wealthy. Nevertheless, the name Calderón was a prominent and well-respected one within the party, whose leaders wanted to continue its growth.

Thus, the PAN put forth Felipe Calderón, a Harvard graduate and conservative politician, as its nominee for the 2006 presidential elections. His opponents were the PRI's Roberto Madrazo, who did not present much of a challenge, and the PRD's candidate Andrés Manuel López Obrador, who had strong support in the poor southern states.

A TESTY, TENSE CAMPAIGN

Some members of the PAN, including President Vicente Fox Quesada, did not support their party's choice for the nomination. Perhaps their reluctance was due to Calderón's personality, which tended to be soft-spoken, in contrast to Obrador's more colorful style and vitality. Obrador was also a champion of the people, having participated and even led on several populist issues on behalf of the poor, and having served as mayor of Mexico City to high approval ratings. In short, he was something of a political celebrity.

However, Calderón's campaign focused on attacking Obrador as a way of gaining support. Foster wrote that the ads "depicted Lopez Obrador, with his broad support from grassroots organizations and the poor, as akin to the radical populist President Hugo Chavez of Venezuela and a danger to the Mexican nation." Indeed, they bluntly stated "Lopez Obrador is a danger to Mexico," according to the BBC's "Profile: Felipe Calderón." These ads were eventually pulled off the air for their defamatory nature, but bad publicity was directed at the PRD's

After decades of enduring corruption and crooked politicians, the Mexican people elected Felipe Calderón, a man who promised to build a better future for the country. During his campaign, Calderón assured the public of his honesty and readiness to maintain order by holding out his hands and saying, "Clean hands, firm hands."

candidate in other ways. When Obrador did not participate in a televised presidential debate, an empty chair was placed on stage to signify his absence.

Calderón's message was "clean hands, firm hands." During speeches on the campaign trail, he would hold out his palms to the audience and declare that they were clean of corruption and that they would govern firmly when it came to cracking down on crime. He also pledged to be firm with the United States and insist on legal residence status for Mexicans living there, as well as opposition to the proposal of building a wall along the U.S.–Mexico border to bar illegal immigration, according to "Profile: Felipe Calderón."

For his part, Obrador claimed that Calderón grew up rich and did not understand the struggles of everyday Mexicans, especially the poor. Many who know Calderón, however, dispute this allegation, pointing to the fact that his upbringing was modest and that he lived the childhood of the average Mexican.

Obrador also struck at Calderón's "clean hands" message, charging him with corruption. When Calderón was secretary of energy, Obrador's campaign alleged, he awarded contracts to the Hildebrando software company, which his brother-in-law owned. Calderón denied the charge, as well as charges that Hildebrando evaded taxes.

Obrador also claimed that Calderón was responsible in part for the Fobaproa problem. In 1994, the government faced an economic crisis, and its response was a program called Fobaproa, which saved many private banks and other elements of the economy. It was a controversial move, though those who supported it claimed that it saved Mexico from financial ruin at a critical time. Critics charge that Fobaproa became an opportunity for corrupt government officials to fatten their wallets even more. Obrador's campaign claimed, furthermore, that the corruption via Fobaproa was arranged by Calderón himself. Calderón did vote for the Fobaproa program, but he insisted that he had nothing to do with corruption.

On election day, July 2, 2006, the election board called the race too close to be determined. The next morning, however, it was made public that Calderón had a small lead of 1.04 percent. However, both Obrador and Calderón declared victory. For a few days, Mexico held its breath; on July 6, the election board announced the official results, which showed that Calderón's margin of victory was even slimmer: 0.58 percent

MANY THINGS CONSPIRED TO MAKE CALDERÓN'S FIRST FEW DAYS AS PRESIDENT DIFFICULT.

(later changed to 0.56 percent), a little over 200,000 votes in an election in which over 40 million people had cast votes. Mexico seemed to erupt in to what Jeremy Schwartz, in "Mexico Strives for Gentler Elections," called the "summer of rebellion."

Obrador's campaign demanded a recount because of alleged fraud and irregularities at some polling stations. The election board, however, allowed only a recount of a fraction of the vote, calling a total recount unnecessary. The tribunal, the judiciary body that reviewed the case, declared Calderón unanimously the victor of the race, but Obrador promised to make Calderón's six years in the presidency very difficult. Many people felt, despite the election board's and the tribunal's reviews, that fraud had taken place nonetheless and that once again, Mexico had reverted to its old ways of political corruption.

At 9:50 A.M. on December 1, 2006, Calderón entered the congressional Chamber of Deputies, the Palacio de San Lazaro, and took the oath of office (having been semiofficially sworn in the night before on national television by Fox), while PRD supporters shouted "Felipe will fall" inside the chambers and Obrador led a demonstration of 100,000 in protest nearby. Ten minutes later, he was out the door in the most contested presidential inauguration in anyone's recent memory. Police barred protestors from demonstrating in front of the Auditoria Nacional, from where Calderón was later scheduled to deliver a speech to a crowd of supporters.

Many things conspired to make Calderón's first few days as president difficult, including the fact, which was a very public one, that Vicente Fox had originally supported another candidate for the PAN nomination. Therefore, Calderón did not even have the legitimate support of Mexico's standing president during his campaign. Obrador's popularity was yet another problem, and the problems with the election and charges of fraud proved more troubling.

Nevertheless, Calderón—who, at 44 years old, was Mexico's youngest president—began his term in office with the goal of restoring trust among the Mexican people, even among the millions who considered him a thief of political office.

A MAN OF RESULTS

Mexicans were placed in an interesting position in the days and weeks after the inauguration of Calderón: they had a new president about whom very little was known. Those who had fully expected Obrador to win were especially curious to know what kind of president Calderón would be, because he was quiet and unassuming, unlike the charismatic and magnanimous Vicente Fox. In fact, Calderón was nicknamed "the young grandpa" for a while.

Those who knew Calderón spoke to the press about his character and style. An article in *The San Diego Tribune* quoted Soledad Loaeza, a political science professor at a local Mexican university, as describing Calderón as persistent and disciplined. This may have surprised many who saw him as a conservative, quiet person who neither steps out of line nor disturbs the status quo. Many people, included Loaeza, also admitted that Calderón's quiet nature had its positive aspects: "He is accustomed to negotiating. He is a person who places importance on the Congress," Loaeza said. This point may well help Calderón, especially since the plans of his predecessor Vicente Fox were often blocked by Congress. Alejandro Poire, a professor of Latin American Studies at Harvard, noted that Calderón would probably try to extend a hand to the PRI by putting PRI people in key political posts.

In the same article, Juan Gabriel Valencia, a PRI congressman who worked with Calderón, said, "I saw him demonstrate very sensible attitudes in legislative negotiations . . . He was a

When Felipe Calderón was announced the winner of the 2006 presidential election, Andrés Manuel López Obrador and his supporters demanded a recount and accused Calderón of fraud *(above)*. Even after an election tribunal declared Calderón the clear winner, though by a slim margin, Obrador refused to accept the ruling and unofficially swore himself in as president.

man who was prepared to look for solutions without worrying about partisan phobias."

Calderón himself hoped to quell much of the criticism that followed the unorthodox election by proving to the nation that he was a steady, stable leader who could restore order. Some critics, however, warned gloomily that, because of the problems with the election, Calderón might have trouble winning the two-thirds of the Senate and the lower house of Congress to pass many of the bills and policies he proposed.

ELECTION MAKEOVER

One positive outcome of the 2006 elections was the attention it drew to the need for election reform. Electoral officials began to worry that they would have another contested election to deal with in 2012 and began working to make sure that would not happen.

Many changes were implemented in the process, and most Mexican states have approved them. Jeremy Schwartz noted in his article, "Mexico Strives for Gentler Elections," that the reforms include changes that resemble European elections. "The next presidential election," he noted, "will last only 90 days. Paid TV and radio ads will be banned, and Mexico's election authority will try to regulate the negativity out of Mexican politics." In 2006, paid advertisements on radio and TV accounted for 70 percent of the $350 million that both parties spent altogether, Schwartz reported. Ads by special interest groups will also be banned, while candidates will be given almost an hour of free airtime by the major stations in order to make the campaigns more fair. Some people applaud the measures, claiming they will allow voters to focus on the candidates' messages and views on the issues, reported Schwartz, but "others have worried the changes, instead of advancing Mexican democracy, represent a return to the authoritarian past. . . . Some analysts say that the ban on advertising could bring back the days when political parties paid journalists under the table for favorable reporting."

In Schwartz's article, political writer Alfonso Zarate said, "Today the incentive to operate in darkness will be greater. . . . The media will still have the power to create or destroy images; they will continue to decide which issues and political personalities to cover." Indeed, the television and radio companies in Mexico have already begun to protest this measure vehemently because their revenue from the elections is in danger.

C H A P T E R

8

Calderón's Challenges

CALDERÓN GREW UP IN THE PAN PARTY BECAUSE OF HIS FATHER'S
influence. Carlos Luken, in an article called "Felipe Calderón:
Mexico's Rising Political Star," wrote, "Because of his father's
image as a strong conservative, for years Calderón was inac-
curately identified as a party purist, and labeled at times a
fundamentalist." This was yet another reason why some in his
own party, including former president Fox, did not support
him at first.

However, as Luken added, "He is to be sure a traditionalist
who does not conform his ideology to suit a political agenda,
but unlike some party notables of earlier times he has demonstrated considerable insight by staying the party's course as it
moved towards new frontiers by allowing renowned business-
men with comparable political agendas to enter and gain direct
access to the party's leadership."

Some critics bring up the point that Calderón's own father would not like the PAN as it has evolved today and recall that Luis Calderón left the PAN later in his life. However, his son —and his other children—always believed in the party, even as it became just as friendly to big business as it was to the Catholic Church. Felipe Calderón's philosophy, as some have summarized it, is the "trickle down" theory; in other words, by helping the wealthy in society, their wealth would trickle down to the rest of society in the form of jobs and a stronger, more stable economy.

As a president who is, in many ways, not what his own party expects of him, Calderón is sure to face many challenges in his administration. But as Juan Gabriel Valencia was quoted in *The San Diego Tribune*, "He will be a president who is distant from the masses, who will be perceived as isolated, without a public image that excites public opinion." Valencia added, "But he can compensate for that with results. And he is a man of results."

In his first two years in office, Calderón has demonstrated that he can indeed achieve results, though not everyone agrees if those results are positive or negative for Mexico.

IMMIGRATION TO THE UNITED STATES

One of the disappointments of Vicente Fox's administration was his inability to negotiate a deal with U.S. president George W. Bush regarding illegal immigrants, despite a promising start. The terror attacks of September 11, 2001, made the U.S. government much more cautious about immigration issues, especially about the vulnerability of the U.S.–Mexico border. It is estimated that 12 million immigrants, mostly Mexican, are in the United States illegally and that half a million more cross into the United States every year to take advantage of job opportunities, according to the BBC in "Q&A: US Immigration Debate." In recent years, more and more of those immigrants

"THE ONLY WAY TO REDUCE IMMIGRATION IS TO CREATE JOBS IN MEXICO."

come from Mexico's southern states, the poorest region in the country.

A few months after taking office, in March 2007, Felipe Calderón discussed the issue of immigration with President George W. Bush. The U.S. government, at that time, had been considering the idea of building a wall, 700 feet (1,126.5 kilometers) in length, along the Mexican border in order to halt immigration. As of 2008, construction on part of that wall was already underway. Indeed, immigration is a key issue in the United States and has been for some time, and most politicians are seeking answers.

During the 2007 talks between the two leaders, Calderón took a firm stance with Bush, insisting that working with Mexico as a partner would be more effective than building walls of separation between the two nations. Before he was elected, Calderón stated, "I think it's a mistake to believe that immigration will be solved by the National Guard or a new wall. The only way to reduce immigration is to create jobs in Mexico," according to a *Washington Post* article, "A Talk with Felipe Calderón."

Time will tell how the immigration issue will play out, especially since Bush's term expires in January 2009 and a new president will be in the White House. Calderón will have to wait and see who his new counterpart in the United States will be and how willing that person will be to tackle immigration.

Calderón is not waiting on the sidelines, however. In February 2008, he made his first official visit to the United States as the Mexican president. While he had no official meetings scheduled with President Bush, Calderón planned to give speeches in several U.S. cities to highlight the issue of

Despite warning President George W. Bush that building a wall on the border between Mexico and the United States would not prevent illegal immigration, construction for a high-security wall went underway. It remains to be seen whether Calderón can influence the next U.S. president's views on immigration.

immigration and to make it a major point in the U.S. presidential election. Many candidates for U.S. president spotlighted immigration in their campaigns, especially Republican candidates who promised potential voters that they would crack down on illegal immigrants.

Calderón has said publicly that he believes Mexican immigrants in the United States are being made scapegoats in the campaign debates so that candidates can seem tougher on security issues. For example, Tom Tancredo, a U.S. representative from Colorado, made immigration reform a central theme of his campaign (though he eventually withdrew from the presidential race). Some of his television commercials were highly controversial and linked illegal immigrants to violence and terrorism in the United States. Critics of Tancredo called these scare tactics and pointed out that most immigrants who come to the United States illegally are simply seeking work opportunities. Mexicans hope that the next U.S. president will have an open mind when it comes to the issue of illegal immigrants within U.S. borders.

"My hope is that whoever the next president is, and whoever is in the new [U.S.] Congress, will have a broader and more comprehensive view" of immigration, Calderón said in a *Los Angeles Times* article by Héctor Tobar. However, he added that he thinks the American people will not allow a president with a radical view against Mexican immigrants into the White House. "It seems to me that the most radical and anti-immigrant candidates have been left behind and have been put in their place by their own electorate," Calderón said, according to Tobar.

"I am especially worried about the growing harassment and frank persecution of Mexicans in the United States in recent days," Calderón informed his country's migrant assistance agency. His comment referred to the uproar caused in Mexico upon learning that U.S. Border Patrol agents were using tear gas against migrants. There is also a sense among Mexicans that their fellow nationals living and working in the United States suffer from discrimination and harassment.

Calderón has ordered Mexican consuls in the United States to work hard to promote the positive contributions of Mexican immigrants. "The key is to neutralize this strategy of confrontation and discrimination that forms part of U.S. society's mistaken perception," said Calderón, according to an MSNBC.com article, "Mexico's Calderón Aims at U.S. campaign."

Writer James C. McKinley Jr. reported on Calderón's strategy: "Calderón said he finds the recent immigrant bashing in American society deeply troubling. The message he hopes to convey to Mexicans living in the United States is that their government has not abandoned them and will help protect their civil rights, even if they broke the law when they crossed the border."

Calderón hopes to convince the United States to allow more immigrants from Mexico legally within its borders.

ECONOMY

As most presidents of Mexico found, Calderón learned that the economy would be the biggest issue he will face. Mexico consistently lags behind other nations in terms of development, income, and financial stability. A struggling economy also affects many other areas of Mexican life, such as education and health care.

Calderón has begun to tackle this issue, with varying levels of success.

During Calderón's first month as president, the price of corn rose and the prices of tortillas—staples of the Mexican diet—increased significantly. Calderón negotiated the Tortilla Price Stabilization Pact between the government and the tortilla companies, which put a limit on how high prices could rise (no more than 30 percent of the original price). The pact was supposed to protect the poorest people of Mexico, who depend on tortillas as a source of affordable food.

The pact was criticized, however, for many reasons, such as the fact that it accepted a 30 percent increase in the tortilla price. Furthermore, the pact was nonbinding, which meant that companies were not forced to abide by it, and many did

When the price of tortillas, a staple of Mexican food, began to rise, Calderón quickly instituted the Tortilla Price Stabilization Pact to prevent costs from spiraling out of control. Mexico's weak economy makes it more susceptible to fluctuating food costs, which directly affect the poor and working class. Here, trade unionists, farmers, and leftist groups protest the rising cost of corn and tortillas.

not, raising their prices well above 30 percent. Supporters of the pact, however, point out that the price of tortillas in most parts of Mexico did not rise excessively.

Calderón has pushed tourism as a way to boost the Mexican economy. By 2012, he said in early 2008, he hopes to achieve a six-fold increase in investments in the tourism industry. Part of this plan includes improving Mexico's infrastructure to make the country more open and friendly for tourists, and 2007's revenues showed that tourism was indeed on the rise. "Our wish is, of course, not just to keep up, but to increase the rhythm of investment in the sector this year. By 2012 we want Mexico to have private investment in tourism of at least 20 billion dollars," Calderón said, according to Web site Earthtimes.org in "Mexico Pushes Six-Fold Tourism Investment Boost by 2012."

Calderón also announced the establishment of a National Infrastructure Fund, to which the government allotted $25 billion. According to "Mexico to Spend $25 Billion on Infrastructure Building," on NewKarala.com, "We're determined to make Mexico the leader in infrastructure development in Latin America and among the emerging economies," Calderón said. The fund's purpose is to improve the nation's transportation systems (highways, roads, railways, and airports) and its water, irrigation and sanitation systems, and to put environmental protection policies into effect. The goal is to make a big improvement in these areas over the next five years.

UNEMPLOYMENT

One of the country's main issues, related to the economy and emigration, is the rate of unemployment in Mexico. Many Mexicans, especially from the lowest economic classes, flee to the United States because they cannot find work in their own country.

Calderón has attempted to address unemployment, but it has been aimed more at the educated middle class. Calderón developed the First Employment Program, which he promised to do during his campaign for president. The program promises government benefits to companies who hire first-time job seekers, such as recent high school and college graduates, as well as women who have never worked outside of the home before. Clearly, Calderón's program aims to prove to Mexicans that opportunities for work are available at home so that people do not feel compelled to cross the northern border into the United States. The program has been in effect only a short while, so it is uncertain whether it can help regain the confidence of Mexican workers.

Just as important, there is not a specific plan in place to address the needs of the millions of poor peasants in Mexico's southern states, where unemployment and dire poverty are at their highest. Calderón, like Fox, supports free enterprise and few restrictions on the market, policies that tend to impact peasants and land workers in a negative way.

The situation grew worse in early 2008 because the United States, which buys 80 percent of Mexico's exports, was experiencing a recession. Because Mexico's economy is so heavily dependent on that of the United States, Mexican economists were predicting that the recession would affect Mexico in the year to come as well. They worried that unemployment would increase, although Calderón has put measures into place to curb inflation, should Mexico also experience a recession of its own. Bloomberg.com reported that "Calderón is accelerating a program to hire private companies to build roads, ports, airports and other infrastructures to help spur the economy. To help rein in inflation, Calderón brokered an agreement in December with the nation's top retailers, including Wal-Mart de Mexico SAB, to sell food staples such as rice, milk and coffee at discounts through March."

CHAPTER

9

The First Years

ONE OF THE MOST TENSE ISSUES BETWEEN THE UNITED STATES AND Mexico is that of drug cartels, the organizations that transmit illegal drugs, such as heroin, cocaine, and others, across the border into the United States.

In their March 2007 meeting, Bush and Calderón exchanged pointed remarks on the issue of drugs. Calderón vowed to help control drug trafficking in Mexico, but he added that the United States—as the consumer of the drugs—also had a responsibility to meet. "While there is no reduction in demand in your territory," he told Bush, "it will be very difficult to reduce the supply in ours," the *Washington Post* reported.

Nevertheless, Calderón's administration has won some victories in the battle against the drug cartels. Since the start of Calderón's presidency, major drug lords have been arrested and their activities have been stopped. In January 2007, drug cartel organizer Pedro Diaz Parada was arrested; the next day,

Mexico agreed to extradite to the United States several criminals related to drug trafficking who were wanted there to stand trial. Then, a year later, in January 2008, the Mexican military seized Alfredo Beltran Leyva in the city of Culiacan in Mexico's northwest. At the time of his arrest, Beltran Leyva, who is considered a key aide to Joaquin Guzman-Loera, the most wanted drug lord in Mexico, was carrying nearly one million dollars in cash. As part of Guzman's operation, Beltran Leyva, according to the Mexican government, was responsible for "transporting drugs, money laundering, and bribing officials," reported Cyntia Barrera.

Calderón has authorized the Mexican police and military to conduct raids on several known drug holdings. By April 2007, it was reported that since Calderón became president, 1,102 drug dealers had been arrested and 500 million pesos in drug money had been confiscated. Hundreds of automobiles, 2 airplanes, and 15 sea vessels used to traffic and transport drugs had also been confiscated from drug dealers. The Calderón administration claimed that these interventions had prevented over 17 million doses of cocaine, almost 1.5 million doses of marijuana, and over 193 million doses of heroin from being distributed.

Calderón has won praise, in both Mexico and the United States, for his aggressive stance against the drug cartels, which were virtually untouched by previous administrations. The *Houston Chronicle* opined, "Mexico's president, Felipe Calderón, has made a crackdown on criminal gangs the centerpiece of his 13-month-old administration. . . . President Calderón, honest federal police and soldiers, and those who support them deserve America's appreciation for their willingness to engage in the battle."

Calderón hopes that such aggressive measures in preventing drug trafficking will win favor with the United States, with whom Mexico hopes to improve its relations. In early February of 2008, the presidents of both countries discussed

Calderón has vowed to combat drug traffickers in Mexico, but insists the war on drugs is a cooperative effort between the United States and Mexico. Though the Mexican military has managed to confiscate and destroy large amounts of marijuana *(above)*, cocaine, and heroin, the drug trade and violence seem to be increasing in Mexico.

the potential for a joint initiative to stop drug cartels across their borders.

CRIME AND VIOLENCE

Despite the halting of many drug cartel operations, critics have noted that drug-related violence continues to rise. In fact, in some areas, drug-related murders have increased by over 40 percent. In other areas of Mexico where poverty is severe, crime continues to also be a problem. Héctor Tobar of the *Los Angeles Times* wrote, "the most immediate threat Calderón faces is organized crime. Violence linked to drug trafficking has claimed more than 2,000 lives since Calderón took office in December 2006. Despite progress, including the arrest of more than 20,000 organized-crime suspects and huge hauls of illicit drugs and cash, much work remains to be done, Calderón said."

Violence of another sort plagues the Calderón administration. On September 10, 2007, reported the *Economist*, "six explosions ripped through gas pipelines in the state of Veracruz, disrupting oil and natural gas supplies, shutting down factories and forcing thousands from their homes. It was the third such attack in three months, and the most severe. Left-wing rebels claimed responsibility." Some viewed the attacks as a comment by rebels on Calderón's tax initiatives, which have failed to be passed by the Congress.

CRITICISM OF CALDERÓN

In February 2008, Felipe Calderón visited his alma mater, Harvard University, where addressed the Kennedy School and the larger campus about his first year as Mexico's president. The campus community gave him a mixed welcome: Some chanted "viva la Felipe" to show their support of a fellow Harvard graduate, while others took to the streets to protest his policies on everything from free trade to immigrants to the Zapatista uprising.

Calderón, aware of protestors outside the building where he delivered his speech, opened his speech by joking, "If you see dust in the air, no worries, because we are cleaning house right now." He went on to dismiss the protests, perhaps because he has been used to protests since well before he was even inaugurated.

CALDERÓN CONTINUED TO STRESS THAT HIS GOVERNMENT UPHOLDS HUMAN RIGHTS.

During his talk, Calderón stressed the accomplishments of his first year, including his crackdown on drug cartels. He also made another plea, which he has consistently done, to keep the border open for immigrants from Mexico to the United States. To close that border and restrict legal immigration, he said, "is a very, very big mistake," adding that the U.S.-Mexico relationship is a "textbook example" of a country with excess labor ready to meet the needs of a country with excess work.

While many claimed to be impressed by Calderón's low-key and steady manner, nobody could ignore the fact that his visit had sparked so much controversy. Outside the building where he spoke, protestors from several groups mingled together, chanting against his visit and his administration's policies. These groups included the Boston Anti-Authoritarian Movement, Massachusetts Global Action, the Boston May Day Coalition, and the Harvard Students for a Democratic Society. One student said he was protesting Calderón's "stolen election history," while another claimed to be "standing in solidarity with the people of Oaxaca and Chiapas and to protest NAFTA."

Calderón continued to stress that his government upholds human rights, and that free trade and the continuation of NAFTA would only help bolster the Mexican economy, rather than hurt small farmers, as critics claim.

A RELIGIOUS HEAD OF STATE

In 2007, Calderón published an autobiography of his life thus far. It was a thin book, possibly because he is still so young and also because his political career has been such an unadventurous and ordinary one. The autobiography was entitled *The Disobedient Son*. The title is a reference to a Mexican folk

An alumnus of Harvard University's John F. Kennedy School of Government, Calderón *(above)* recognizes the importance of maintaining positive U.S.-Mexico relations. Because progress in Mexico's economy depends so much on the United States, Calderón promised to work closely with the U.S. government in matters concerning border control, drug trafficking, and immigration.

song of the same title, in which the main character's name is also Felipe. However, some have suggested that Calderón was trying to make a point that he is a rebel because he ran for the position despite the fact that Vicente Fox had favored someone else for the nomination. The irony, of course, is that Calderón's life can hardly be described as that of a rebel or as a disobedient person in any way. He has followed the prescribed and very traditional course of someone who literally was raised in the PAN party and has now risen to its top levels.

Calderón is one of the few Mexican presidents to have a deeply religious upbringing and background. Though he has said he will not, as president, try to make religious doctrine into legislation, he does adhere personally to church teachings. He was satisfied with Mexican laws, for example, that made abortion a crime except in certain cases. In April 2007, when a law was passed that legalized abortion, the PAN tried to block it from being approved. Calderón himself and his secretary of health condemned the legislation.

Throughout his campaign and his first years in office, Calderón has had the support of the church and church officials. In fact, many Mexicans see the PAN as the political party of the Catholic Church, and many oppose it for this reason. Calderón, as a president who openly professes his faith (though he does not discuss it publicly), will have to deal with opposition from secularists.

Surprisingly, for having served in a position that many Mexicans believe he did not legitimately win, Calderón has enjoyed good approval ratings from the population. His approval rating hovers in the mid-range, with a little more than half the population believing he is doing a good job in office. Ironically, despite the controversy of the election and his affiliation with and support from the church, Calderón is generally viewed as an honest president who is working hard to improve the domestic situation in Mexico, such as by being more aggressive in stopping the drug cartels.

CHRONOLOGY

1910   Mexican Revolution.

1917   Constitution of 1917 includes land reforms to uphold the rights of the peasants and lower classes, including indigenous Indians, and laws prohibiting the powers of the Catholic Church.

1929   Plutarco Elías Calles founds the National Revolutionary Party, which later becomes the PRI.

1940   Lázaro Cárdenas is first president since the revolution to leave office peacefully and transition power smoothly to the next president.

1954   Mexican women win the right to vote.

1962   Felipe Calderón born to Maria del Carmen Hinojosa Calderón and Luis Calderón Vega

1988   The presidential election prompts charges of fraud by the PRI; Mexicans grow more dissatisfied with the PRI.

1989   In the gubernatorial elections, a non-PRI governor wins for the first time in 50 years.

1993   Mexico, the United States, and Canada sign the highly controversial NAFTA agreement, allowing for eventual free trade among the three nations.

1994   PRI leader José Ruiz Massieu is assassinated.

1995   Scandal for PRI, as assassination of Ruiz Massieu involves Raul Salinas, former president Carlos Salinas de Gortari's brother.

1996   Calderón serves as president of PAN until 1999.

1997	Opposition parties win enough seats in Congress to take the majority away from the PRI.
2000	Vicente Fox Quesada of the PAN is first non-PRI president elected in over 70 years.
2001	Terrorist attacks on the United States cause problems for Fox's plans to negotiate immigration issues with its northern neighbor.
2006	Felipe Calderón wins presidential election by a slim margin, among charges of fraud and corruption.
2007	The Calderón administration reports millions of dollars confiscated and hundreds arrested in drug cartels.
2008	Mexican economists announce an expected dip in the economy because of a recession being experienced by the United States.
2008	Calderón makes his first official visit to the United States.

BIBLIOGRAPHY

Baker, Peter. "Calderón Admonishes Bush on Thorny Issues." *Washington Post*. March 14, 2007. Available online. http://www.washingtonpost.com/wp-dyn/content/article/2007/03/13/AR2007031300169.html.

Barrera, Cyntia. "Mexico Arrests Senior Drug Cartel Member." Reuters.com. January 22, 2008. Retrieved January 26, 2008. Available online. http://www.reuters.com/article/newsOne/idUSN2139879720080122

Camp, Roderic Ai, and Colin MacLachlan. "Mexico." Microsoft Encarta Online Encyclopedia 2007. Retrieved December 31, 2007. Available online. http://encarta.msn.com.

Dickinson, Terri. "The Plan de Iguala." Historical Text Archive. Retrieved December 20, 2007. Available online. http://www.historicaltextarchive.com/sections.php?op=viewarticle&artid=538.

Ecker, Ronald. "The Tlatelolco Massacre in Mexico." The Ron Ecker Home Page. August 15, 2007. Retrieved December 5, 2007. Available online. http://www.ronaldecker.com/massacre.htm.

Fedarko, Kevin. "The Spreading Scandal." *Time*. March 13, 1995. Retrieved December 5, 2007. Available online. http://www.time.com/time/magazine/article/0,9171,982680-2,00.html.

Foster, Lynn V. *A Brief History of Mexico*. Revised edition. New York: Facts On File, 2004.

Hamnett, Brian R. *A Concise History of Mexico*. 2nd Edition. New York: Cambridge University Press, 2006.

"Hernán Cortés Arrives in Mexico." PBS.org. Retrieved December 26, 2007. Available online. http://www.pbs.org/kpbs/theborder/history/timeline/1.html.

"Hernán Cortés, Explorer and Conqueror of Mexico." MEX-Online.com. Retrieved December 27, 2007. Available online. http://www.mexonline.com/hernan-cortez.htm.

Hider, James. "Mexican Inauguration Erupts into Fistfights." *Times* Online. December 1, 2006. Retrieved November 7, 2007. Available online. http://www.timesonline.co.uk/tol/news/world/us_and_americas/article657390.ece.

Jordan, Mary. "In Mexico, Church's Influence Wanes as Evangelism Grows." *Washington Post.* April 5, 2005. Retrieved February 12, 2008. Available online. http://www.washingtonpost.com/wp-dyn/articles/A26323-2005Apr4.html.

Lacey, Marc. "Felipe Calderón: A Politician at Birth." *New York Times.* September 6, 2006. Retrieved October 2, 2007. Available online. http://www.nytimes.com/2006/09/06/world/americas/06calderon.html.

Luken, Carlos. "Felipe Calderón: Mexico's Rising Political Star." October 10, 2005. Mexidata.info. Retrieved February 1, 2008. Available online. http://mexidata.info/id633.html.

McKinley, James C., Jr. "Mexican Leader's Visit to US Avoids DC." MercuryNews.com. February 9, 2008. Retrieved February 9, 2008. Available online. http://www.mercurynews.com/ci_8815795?source=rss.

"Mexico's Calderón Aims at U.S. Campaign." MSNBC.com. February 8, 2008. Retrieved February 9, 2008. Available online. http://www.msnbc.msn.com/id/23074668/

"Mexico to Spend $25bn on Infrastructure Building." NewKerala.com. February 8, 2008. Retrieved February 9, 2008. Available online. http://www.newkerala.com/one.php?action=fullnews&id=20226.

"Mexico Pushes Six-Fold Tourism Investment Boost by 2012." Earthtimes.org. February 7, 2008. Retrieved February 9,

2008. Available online. http://www.earthtimes.org/articles/show/184368,mexico-pushes-six-fold-tourism-investment-boost-by-2012.html.

"Mexico's Teetering President." *Economist.* September 13, 2007. Retrieved October 5, 2007. Available online. http://www.economist.com/world/la/displaystory.cfm?story_id=9804502.

"Mexico's War: President Calderón Deserves Credit for Getting Serious in the Battle Against Bloody Drug Cartels." *Houston Chronicle.* January 29, 2008. Retrieved February 6, 2008. Available online. http://www.chron.com/disp/story.mpl/editorial/5496851.html.

Miller, Robert Ryal. "The War Between the United States and Mexico." PBS.org. Retrieved December 31, 2007. Available online. http://www.pbs.org/kera/usmexicanwar/aftermath/war.html.

"Profile: Felipe Calderón." BBC News. September 5, 2006. Retrieved October 10, 2007. Available online. http://news.bbc.co.uk/2/hi/americas/5318434.stm.

"Q&A: US Immigration Debate." BBC News. June 28, 2007. Retrieved January 10, 2008. Available online. http://news.bbc.co.uk/2/hi/americas/4850634.stm.

Ross, John. "Calderón Installed by Media and Military: Repression on the Menu in Mexico." Counterpunch.org. December 4, 2006. Retrieved November 7, 2007. Available online. http://www.counterpunch.org/ross12042006.html.

Rota, Valerie, and Jens Erik Gould. "Mexico Slashes 2008 Growth Forecast on U.S. Economy." Bloomberg.com. February 5, 2008. Retrieved on February 6, 2008. Available online. http://www.bloomberg.com/apps/news?pid=newsarchive&sid=aS0b4e0yVJ6Q.

Schwartz, Jeremy. "Mexico Strives for Gentler Elections." Boston.com. September 30, 2007. Retrieved October 5, 2007. Available online. http://www.boston.com/news/world/articles/2007/09/30/mexico_strives_for_gentler_elections/.

Suchlicki, Jaime. *Mexico: From Montezuma to the Fall of the PRI.* 2nd edition. Washington, DC: Potomac Books, 2001.

"A Talk with Felipe Calderón." *Washington Post.* June 18, 2006. Retrieved November 10, 2007. Available online. http://www.washingtonpost.com/wp-dyn/content/article/2006/06/17/AR2006061700569.html.

Thompson, Ginger. "Ex-President in Mexico Casts New Light on Rigged 1988 Election." *New York Times.* March 9, 2004. Retrieved December 1, 2007. Available online. http://query.nytimes.com/gst/fullpage.html?res=9C05E3DD173EF93AA35750C0A9629C8B63&scp=1&sq=Ex-President+in+Mexico+Casts+New+Light+on+Rigged+1988+Election&st=nyt.

Tobar, Héctor. "Mexican President Foresees Friendlier U.S." *Los Angeles Times.* February 7, 2008. Retrieved February 9, 2008. Available online. http://www.latimes.com/news/nationworld/world/la-fg-calderon7feb07,1,5342083.story?track=rss.

Walker, S. Lynne. "Few really know Calderón; his actions will be the key." *The San Diego Tribune.* December 1, 2006. Available online. http://www.signonsandiego.com/uniontrib/20061201/news_1n1calderon.html

"The Zapatista Uprising 1994–2004: A Look at How an Indigenous Rebel Group from Chiapas Took on Mexico and Corporate Globalization." Democracy Now. January 2, 2004. Retrieved January 20, 2008. Available online. http://www.democracynow.org/2004/1/2/the_zapatista_uprising_1994_2004_a.

FURTHER READING

Gritzner, Charles F. *Mexico, Updated Edition.* New York: Chelsea House, 2005.

Joseph, Gilbert M., and Timothy J. Henderson, eds. *The Mexico Reader: History, Culture, Politics.* Durham, NC: Duke University Press, 2002.

Paprocki, Sherry Beck. *Vicente Fox.* New York: Chelsea House, 2002.

Ruggiero, Adriane. *Mexico.* San Diego: Greenhaven Press, 2004.

Tidmarsh, Celia. *Focus on Mexico.* Milwaukee, Wisc: World Almanac Library, 2006.

WEB SITES

All About Mexico. History.com.
http://www.history.com/states.do?parentId=MEXICO

Mexico for Kids. Office of the President of the Republic of Mexico.
http://www.elbalero.gob.mx/index_kids.html

PHOTO CREDITS

INDEX

109

ABOUT THE AUTHORS

SUSAN MUADDI DARRAJ is associate professor of English at Harford Community College in Bel Air, Maryland. She earned her MA in English literature from Rutgers University in Camden, New Jersey. Her book of short fiction, *The Inheritance of Exile*, was published in 2007 by University of Notre Dame Press.

ARTHUR SCHLESINGER, JR. is remembered as the leading American historian of our time. He won the Pulitzer Prize for his books *The Age of Jackson* (1945) and *A Thousand Days* (1965), which also won the National Book Award. Schlesinger was the Albert Schweitzer Professor of the Humanities at the City University of New York and was involved in several other Chelsea House projects, including the series *Revolutionary War Leaders*, *Colonial Leaders*, and *Your Government*.